USBORNE INTERNET-LINKED
GERMAN
DICTIONARY
FOR BEGINNERS

Helen Davies
Illustrated by John Sha(
Designed by Brian Robe.
Edited by Nicole Irving

D1566551

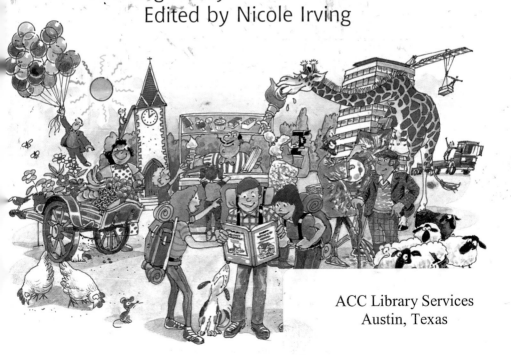

Language consultants: Helga Holtkamp and Anke Kornmüller
Additional designs by Kim Blundell, Stephen Wright and Sarah Cronin
Editorial help from Anita Ganeri and Katie Daynes

Contents

About nouns

German nouns are either masculine, feminine or neuter (this is called their gender). "The" is **der** for a masculine word, **die** for a feminine word and **das** for a neuter word. In the plural, the word for "the" is **die**, whatever the gender of the noun. The following abbreviations are sometimes used to make the gender and number clear: **(f)** feminine, **(m)** masculine, **(n)** neuter, **(s)** singular, **(pl)** plural. In German, nouns that describe what people do or are (e.g. dancer) often have a masculine and a feminine form. Both forms are given in the word list at the back of this book. Look out for letters in brackets after a noun. You add these letters to make the plural form. Sometimes, you also add an umlaut (¨) over the vowel.

About adjectives

German adjectives take different endings depending on the noun they are describing and the job it does in the sentence. You can find out more about this on page 98 of the grammar section. It is best to learn the simple form of the adjective without any ending, so this is the form given in the picture labels and word boxes.

About verbs

Verbs in this book appear in the infinitive (e.g. "to hide" in English). In German, the infinitive always ends in **en**. There are two kinds of German verbs, weak verbs and strong verbs. These verbs have different patterns, which you can read about on page 100 of the grammar section.

2

Usborne Quicklinks

This book has its own Usborne Quicklinks Web site where you can listen to all the words and phrases read by a native German speaker.

To visit the Quicklinks Web site for this book, go to **www.usborne-quicklinks.com** and enter the keywords "german dictionary for beginners".

Listening to the words
To hear the words and phrases in this book, you will need your Web browser (e.g. Internet Explorer or Netscape Navigator) and a program such as RealPlayer® or Windows® Media Player. These programs are free and, if you don't already have one of them, you can download them from Usborne Quicklinks. Your computer also needs a sound card but most computers already have one.

Picture puzzles and useful Web sites
In Usborne Quicklinks you will also find German picture puzzles that you can print out for free, and links to lots of other useful Web sites where you can listen to German radio, improve your German grammar and find out more about the country and culture.

Disclaimer
The Usborne Quicklinks Web site contains links to external Web sites that do not belong to Usborne Publishing. The links are regularly reviewed and updated, but Usborne Publishing is not responsible for the content on any Web site other than its own. We recommend that children are supervised while on the Internet, that they do not use Internet Chat Rooms, and that you use Internet filtering software to block unsuitable material. Please ensure that children read and follow the safety guidelines displayed in Usborne Quicklinks. For more information, see the **Net Help** area on the Usborne Quicklinks Web site.

Meeting people

Hallo

Auf Wiedersehen

Bis bald.

küssen

der Mann

die Frau

das Baby

die Hand schütteln

der Junge

das Mädchen

Hallo	Hello	**der Mann(¨er)**	man
Auf Wiedersehen*	Goodbye	**die Frau(en)**	woman
Bis bald.	See you later.	**das Baby(s)**	baby
die Hand schütteln	to shake hands with	**der Junge(n)**	boy
küssen	to kiss	**das Mädchen(-)**	girl

vorstellen

treffen

Wie geht's?

Danke, gut.

die Freundin

der Freund

vorstellen	to introduce	**Wie geht's?**	How are you?
die Freundin(nen)	friend (f)	**Danke, gut.**	Very well, thank you.
der Freund(e)	friend (m)		
treffen	to meet		

* You can find the literal meaning of phrases and expressions in the Phrase explainer section on pages 106-9.

sich unterhalten	to chat
Ja	Yes
Nein	No
Das meine ich auch.	I agree.
sagen	to say
in Gelächter ausbrechen	to burst out laughing

[C]

der Name(n)	name
der Vorname(n)	first name
der Nachname(n)	surname
Wie heißt du?*	What's your name?
Ich heiße…	My name is…
Er heißt…	His name is…

[D]

das Alter(-)	age	**alt**	old
Wie alt bist du?	How old are you?	**älter als**	older than
Ich bin neunzehn.	I'm nineteen	**jünger als**	younger than
jung	young	**genauso alt wie**	the same age as

[E] [F]

* ß is a German letter which stands for ss.

5

Families

die Familie
der Vater
die Mutter
der Großvater
die Tante
der Onkel
die Großmutter
der Bruder
die Schwester
die Kusine
der Vetter

die **Familie(n)**	family	die **Großmutter(¨)**	grandmother
der **Vater(¨)**	father	die **Tante(n)**	aunt
die **Mutter(¨)**	mother	der **Onkel(-)**	uncle
der **Bruder(¨)**	brother	die **Kusine(n)**	cousin (f)
die **Schwester(n)**	sister	der **Vetter(n)**	cousin (m)
der **Großvater(¨)**	grandfather		

verwandt sein mit
der Sohn
der Enkel
die Tochter
die Enkelin
der Neffe
aufziehen
lieb haben
die Nichte

verwandt sein mit	to be related to	die **Enkelin(nen)**	granddaughter
der **Sohn(¨e)**	son	**lieb haben**	to be fond of
die **Tochter(¨)**	daughter	der **Neffe(n)**	nephew
aufziehen	to bring up	die **Nichte(n)**	niece
der **Enkel(-)**	grandson		

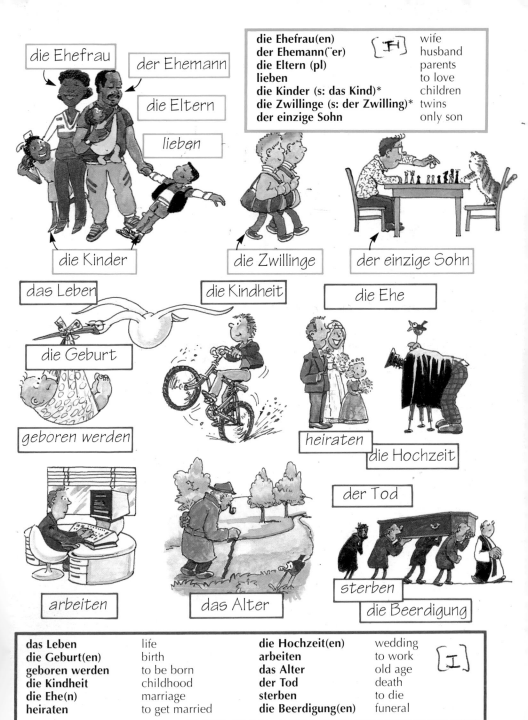

die Ehefrau

der Ehemann

die Eltern

lieben

die Ehefrau(en)		wife
die Ehemann(¨er)		husband
die Eltern (pl)		parents
lieben		to love
die Kinder (s: das Kind)*		children
die Zwillinge (s: der Zwilling)*		twins
der einzige Sohn		only son

die Kinder

die Zwillinge

der einzige Sohn

das Leben

die Kindheit

die Ehe

die Geburt

geboren werden

heiraten

die Hochzeit

der Tod

arbeiten

das Alter

sterben

die Beerdigung

das Leben	life	die Hochzeit(en)	wedding
die Geburt(en)	birth	arbeiten	to work
geboren werden	to be born	das Alter	old age
die Kindheit	childhood	der Tod	death
die Ehe(n)	marriage	sterben	to die
heiraten	to get married	die Beerdigung(en)	funeral

* **Das Kind** and **der Zwilling** are the singular forms.

7

Appearance and personality

hübsch

gutaussehend

hübsch	pretty
gutaussehend	handsome
stark	strong
schwach	weak
dünn	thin
schlank	slim
dick	fat

[J]

stark

dünn

dick

schwach

schlank

blondes Haar haben

eine Glatze haben

braunes Haar

rotes Haar

glattes Haar

Locken

der Pony

die Zöpfe

blondes Haar haben	to have blond hair	**Locken**	curly hair
braunes Haar	brown hair	**der Pony(s)**	a fringe
rotes Haar	red hair	**die Zöpfe (pl)**	plaits
glattes Haar	straight hair	**eine Glatze haben**	to be bald

[K]

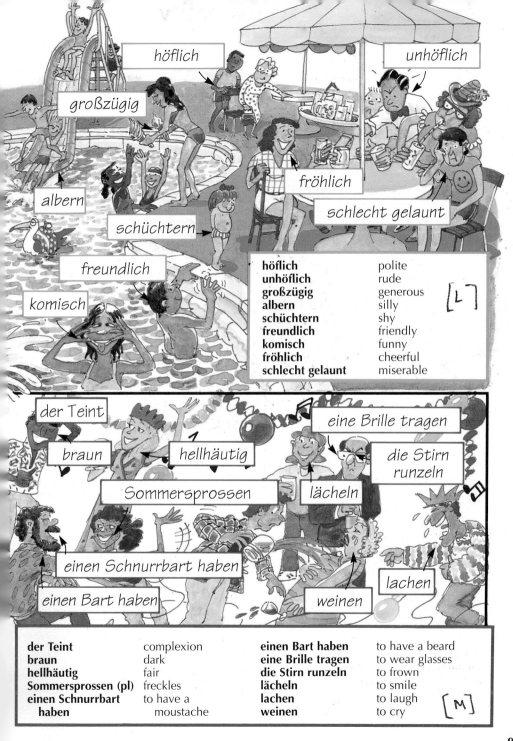

höflich

unhöflich

großzügig

fröhlich

albern

schlecht gelaunt

schüchtern

freundlich

komisch

höflich	polite
unhöflich	rude
großzügig	generous
albern	silly
schüchtern	shy
freundlich	friendly
komisch	funny
fröhlich	cheerful
schlecht gelaunt	miserable

[L]

der Teint

eine Brille tragen

braun

hellhäutig

die Stirn runzeln

Sommersprossen

lächeln

einen Schnurrbart haben

einen Bart haben

lachen

weinen

der Teint	complexion	**einen Bart haben**	to have a beard
braun	dark	**eine Brille tragen**	to wear glasses
hellhäutig	fair	**die Stirn runzeln**	to frown
Sommersprossen (pl)	freckles	**lächeln**	to smile
einen Schnurrbart	to have a	**lachen**	to laugh
haben	moustache	**weinen**	to cry

[M]

Your body

der Kopf(¨e)	head
das Haar(e)	hair
das Gesicht(er)	face
die Haut	skin
das Auge(n)	eye
die Backe(n)	cheek
die Nase(n)	nose
das Ohr(en)	ear
der Mund(¨er)	mouth
der Zahn(¨e)	tooth
die Zunge(n)	tongue
die Lippe(n)	lip
der Hals(¨e)	neck
das Kinn(e)	chin

(N)

der Kopf

das Haar

das Gesicht

die Haut

das Auge

die Backe

die Nase

das Ohr

der Mund

der Zahn

die Zunge

die Lippe

der Hals

das Kinn

der Körper

die Schulter

die Hand

der Finger

der Daumen

das Handgelenk

die Brust

der Arm

der Rücken

der Ellbogen

der Bauch

das Bein

das Knie

der Zeh

der Knöchel

der Fuß

die Ferse

der Körper(-)	body
die Schulter(n)	shoulder
die Brust(¨e)	chest
der Arm(e)	arm
der Ellbogen(-)	elbow
die Hand(¨e)	hand
der Finger(-)	finger
der Daumen(-)	thumb
das Handgelenk(e)	wrist
der Rücken(-)	back
der Bauch(¨e)	stomach
das Bein(e)	leg
das Knie(-)	knee
der Zeh(en)	toe
der Fuß(¨sse)	foot
der Knöchel(-)	ankle
die Ferse(n)	heel

(O)

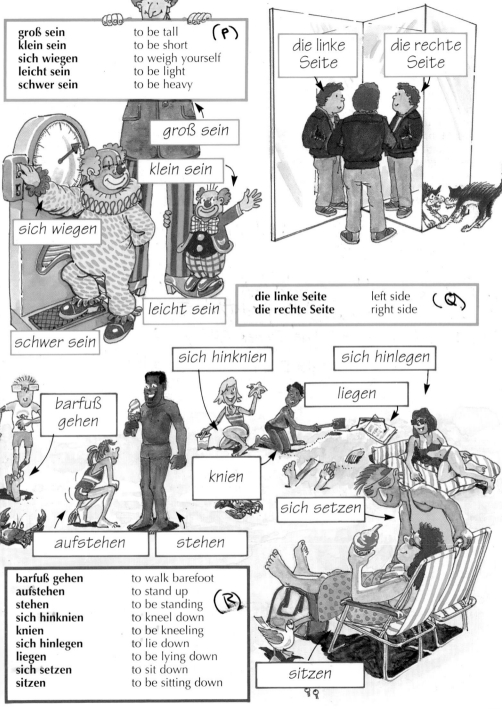

groß sein	to be tall
klein sein	to be short
sich wiegen	to weigh yourself
leicht sein	to be light
schwer sein	to be heavy

(P)

die linke Seite

die rechte Seite

groß sein

klein sein

sich wiegen

leicht sein

schwer sein

die linke Seite	left side
die rechte Seite	right side

sich hinknien

sich hinlegen

liegen

barfuß gehen

knien

sich setzen

aufstehen

stehen

barfuß gehen	to walk barefoot
aufstehen	to stand up
stehen	to be standing
sich hinknien	to kneel down
knien	to be kneeling
sich hinlegen	to lie down
liegen	to be lying down
sich setzen	to sit down
sitzen	to be sitting down

(R)

sitzen

11

Houses and homes

der Wohnblock

die Wohnung

Ich bin zu Hause.

der zweite Stock

die Wohnungstür

die Klingel

klingeln

der Briefkasten

die Fußmatte

der Balkon

der Hausmeister

einziehen

das Erdgeschoss

das Haus

in einem Haus wohnen

die Nachbarin

die Eigentümerin

ausziehen

der erste Stock

der Mieter

das Untergeschoss

der Wohnblock(s)	block of apartments
die Wohnung(en)	apartment
Ich bin zu Hause.	I'm at home.
der zweite Stock	second floor
die Wohnungstür(en)	front door
die Klingel(n)	doorbell
klingeln	to ring the bell
der Briefkasten(¨)	letter box
die Fußmatte(n)	doormat
der Balkon(s)	balcony
der erste Stock	first floor
der Hausmeister(-)	caretaker (m)
einziehen	to move in
das Erdgeschoss(e)	ground floor

das Haus(¨er)	house
in einem Haus wohnen	to live in a house
die Nachbarin(nen)	neighbour (f)
die Eigentümerin(nen)	landlady
ausziehen	to move out
der Mieter(-)	tenant (m)
das Untergeschoss(e)	basement

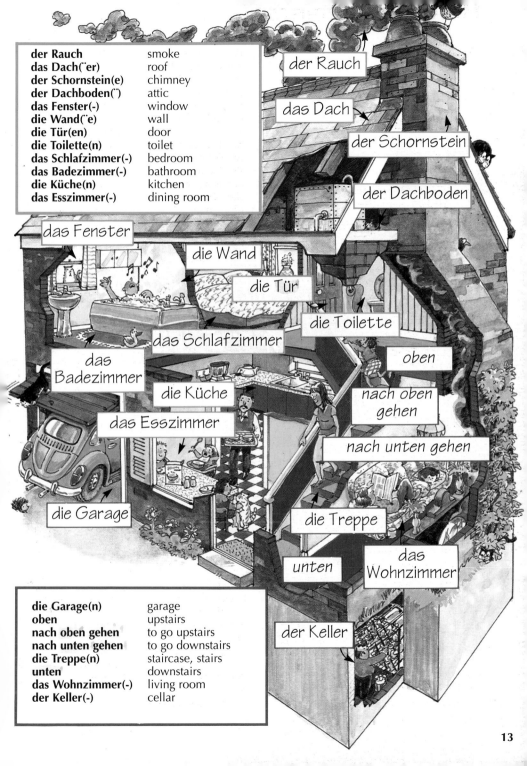

der Rauch	smoke
das Dach(¨er)	roof
der Schornstein(e)	chimney
der Dachboden(¨)	attic
das Fenster(-)	window
die Wand(¨e)	wall
die Tür(en)	door
die Toilette(n)	toilet
das Schlafzimmer(-)	bedroom
das Badezimmer(-)	bathroom
die Küche(n)	kitchen
das Esszimmer(-)	dining room

der Rauch

das Dach

der Schornstein

der Dachboden

das Fenster

die Wand

die Tür

die Toilette

das Schlafzimmer

oben

das Badezimmer

die Küche

nach oben gehen

das Esszimmer

nach unten gehen

die Garage

die Treppe

das Wohnzimmer

unten

der Keller

die Garage(n)	garage
oben	upstairs
nach oben gehen	to go upstairs
nach unten gehen	to go downstairs
die Treppe(n)	staircase, stairs
unten	downstairs
das Wohnzimmer(-)	living room
der Keller(-)	cellar

Dining room and living room

das **Esszimmer**(-)	dining room
die **Lampe**(n)	light
der **Heizkörper**(-)	radiator
der **Tisch**(e)	table
der **Stuhl**(¨e)	chair
der **Fußboden**(¨)	floor
der **Teppich**(e)	carpet

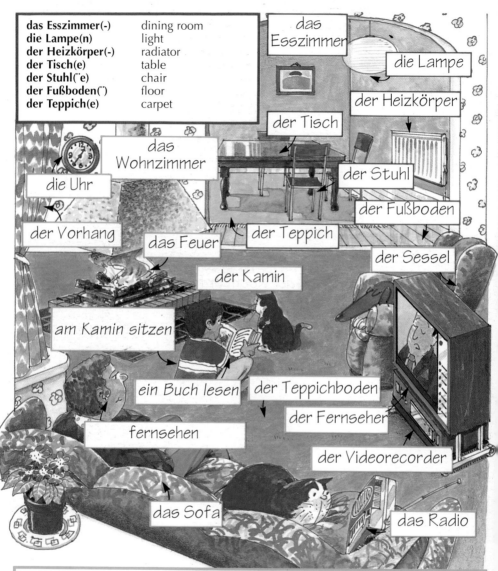

das Esszimmer

die Lampe

der Heizkörper

der Tisch

der Stuhl

der Fußboden

das Wohnzimmer

die Uhr

der Vorhang

das Feuer

der Teppich

der Sessel

der Kamin

am Kamin sitzen

ein Buch lesen

der Teppichboden

der Fernseher

fernsehen

der Videorecorder

das Sofa

das Radio

das **Wohnzimmer**(-)	living room	das **Sofa**(s)	sofa
die **Uhr**(en)	clock	**fernsehen**	to watch television
der **Vorhang**(¨e)	curtain	der **Teppichboden**(¨)	wall-to-wall carpet
das **Feuer**(-)	fire	der **Fernseher**(-)	television
der **Kamin**(e)	fireplace	der **Videorecorder**(-)	VCR (video cassette recorder)
der **Sessel**(-)	armchair		
am Kamin sitzen	to sit by the fire	das **Radio**(s)	radio
ein Buch lesen	to read a book		

14

In the kitchen

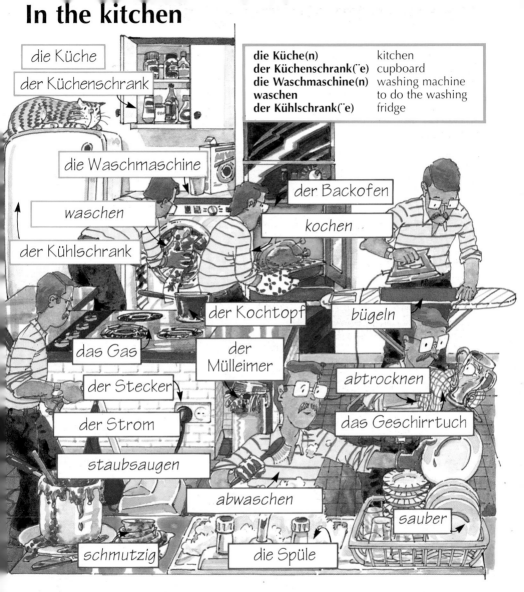

die Küche

der Küchenschrank

die Waschmaschine

waschen

der Kühlschrank

der Backofen

kochen

der Kochtopf

bügeln

das Gas

der Mülleimer

der Stecker

abtrocknen

der Strom

das Geschirrtuch

staubsaugen

abwaschen

sauber

schmutzig

die Spüle

die Küche(n)	kitchen
der Küchenschrank(¨e)	cupboard
die Waschmaschine(n)	washing machine
waschen	to do the washing
der Kühlschrank(¨e)	fridge

der Backofen(¨)	oven	staubsaugen	to vacuum
kochen	to cook	abwaschen	to do the dishes
der Kochtopf(¨e)	saucepan	schmutzig	dirty
das Gas	gas	die Spüle(n)	sink
der Mülleimer(-)	waste basket	abtrocknen	to dry, to wipe
bügeln	to iron	das Geschirrtuch(¨er)	tea towel
der Stecker(-)	plug	sauber	clean
der Strom	electricity		

15

In the garden

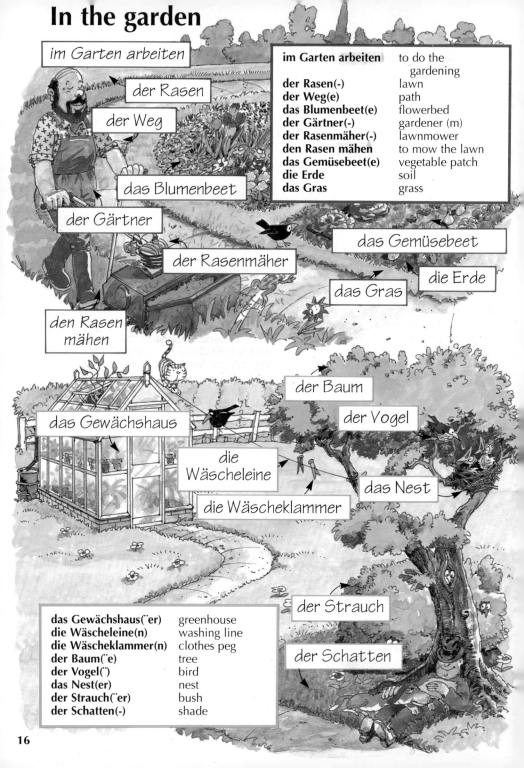

im Garten arbeiten

der Rasen

der Weg

das Blumenbeet

der Gärtner

der Rasenmäher

den Rasen mähen

im Garten arbeiten	to do the gardening
der Rasen(-)	lawn
der Weg(e)	path
das Blumenbeet(e)	flowerbed
der Gärtner(-)	gardener (m)
der Rasenmäher(-)	lawnmower
den Rasen mähen	to mow the lawn
das Gemüsebeet(e)	vegetable patch
die Erde	soil
das Gras	grass

das Gemüsebeet

die Erde

das Gras

der Baum

der Vogel

das Gewächshaus

die Wäscheleine

die Wäscheklammer

das Nest

der Strauch

der Schatten

das Gewächshaus(¨er)	greenhouse
die Wäscheleine(n)	washing line
die Wäscheklammer(n)	clothes peg
der Baum(¨e)	tree
der Vogel(¨)	bird
das Nest(er)	nest
der Strauch(¨er)	bush
der Schatten(-)	shade

die Biene

der Schmetterling

die Rose

duftend

bunt

die Wespe

stechen

die Dahlie

die Geranie

die Tulpe

die Osterglocke

das Vergissmeinnicht

der Blumensamen

das Unkraut

pflanzen

die Blumenzwiebel

Unkraut jäten

die Biene(n)	bee	**die Tulpe(n)**	tulip
der Schmetterling(e)	butterfly	**das Vergissmeinnicht(-)**	forget-me-not
die Wespe(n)	wasp	**die Osterglocke(n)**	daffodil
stechen	to sting	**der Blumensamen(-)**	seed
die Rose(n)	rose	**pflanzen**	to plant
duftend	sweet-smelling	**die Blumenzwiebel(n)**	bulb
bunt	colorful	**Unkraut jäten**	to weed
die Dahlie(n)	dahlia	**das Unkraut(ˉer)**	weed
die Geranie(n)	geranium		

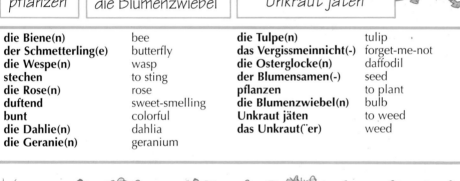

das Gartenhäuschen

der Spaten

die Gabel

die Gießkanne

die Schubkarre

die Schaufel

die Harke

das Gartenhäuschen(-)	garden shed
die Schubkarre(n)	wheelbarrow
die Schaufel(n)	trowel
die Harke(n)	rake
der Spaten(-)	spade
die Gabel(n)	fork
die Gießkanne(n)	watering can

Pets

der Hund(e)	dog
die Hundehütte(n)	kennel
der junge Hund	puppy
das Fell	fur
die Pfote(n)	paw
verspielt	playful
bellen	to bark
VORSICHT BISSIGER HUND!	BEWARE OF THE DOG!
jagen	to chase
bringen	to fetch
der Schwanz(¨e)	tail
mit dem Schwanz wedeln	to wag its tail
knurren	to growl
den Hund ausführen	to take the dog for a walk

der Hund

die Hundehütte

der junge Hund

das Fell

die Pfote

verspielt

bellen

VORSICHT BISSIGER HUND!

jagen

knurren

bringen

der Schwanz

mit dem Schwanz wedeln

den Hund ausführen

die Katze(n)	cat
der Korb(¨e)	basket
schnurren	to purr
das Kätzchen(-)	kitten
miauen	to mew
sich strecken	to stretch
die Kralle(n)	claw
weich	soft
süß	sweet

die Katze

der Korb

schnurren

das Kätzchen

miauen

weich

sich strecken

die Kralle

süß

der Wellensittich(e)	parrot	das Kaninchen(-)	rabbit
hocken	to perch	die Schildkröte(n)	tortoise
der Flügel(-)	wing	der Käfig(e)	cage
der Schnabel(¨)	beak	füttern	to feed
die Feder(n)	feather	der Goldfisch(e)	goldfish
der Hamster(-)	hamster	die Maus(¨e)	mouse
der Igel(-)	hedgehog	das Goldfischglas(¨er)	goldfish bowl
das Meerschweinchen(-)	guinea pig		

der Wellensittich
der Flügel
der Hamster
hocken
der Schnabel
die Feder
der Igel
das Meerschweinchen
das Kaninchen
die Schildkröte
der Käfig
füttern
der Goldfisch
die Maus
das Goldfischglas

Getting up

aufwachen

Guten Morgen

sich die Augen reiben

gähnen

der Wecker

aufwachen	to wake up
Guten Morgen	Good-morning
sich die Augen reiben	to rub your eyes
gähnen	to yawn
der Wecker(-)	alarm clock

aufstehen

die Vorhänge aufziehen

aufstehen	to get up
die Vorhänge aufziehen	to open the curtains
der Morgenmantel(¨)	robe

der Morgenmantel

die Dusche

duschen

sich die Haare waschen

das Shampoo

die Dusche(n)	shower
duschen	to have a shower
sich die Haare waschen	to wash your hair
das Shampoo(s)	shampoo
sich waschen	to wash, to have a wash
die Seife(n)	soap
der Waschlappen(-)	washcloth
sich abtrocknen	to dry yourself
das Handtuch(¨er)	towel
nackt	naked

sich abtrocknen

das Handtuch

sich waschen

die Seife

der Waschlappen

nackt

sich rasieren	to shave
der Spiegel(-)	mirror
der elektrische	electric shaver
Rasierapparat(e)	
der Rasierapparat(e)	razor
der Rasierschaum	shaving foam

sich rasieren

der Spiegel

der elektrische Rasierapparat

der Rasierapparat

der Rasierschaum

heißes Wasser

kaltes Wasser

der Wasserhahn

die Zahnpasta

die Zahnbürste

sich die Zähne putzen

der Wasserhahn(¨e)	tap
heißes Wasser	hot water
kaltes Wasser	cold water
die Zahnpasta	toothpaste
die Zahnbürste(n)	toothbrush
sich die Zähne putzen	to clean your teeth

sich die Haare fönen	to dry your hair
der Fön(s)	hairdrier
die Haarbürste(n)	brush
der Kamm(¨e)	comb
sich die Haare kämmen	to comb your hair
sich die Haare bürsten	to brush your hair

sich die Haare fönen

der Fön

die Haarbürste

der Kamm

sich schminken

die Wimperntusche

sich die Haare kämmen

sich die Haare bürsten

das Make-up

der Lippenstift

das Parfüm

sich schminken	to put on make-up
die Wimperntusche(n)	mascara
das Make-up(s)	foundation cream
der Lippenstift(e)	lipstick
das Parfüm(s)	perfume

Clothes

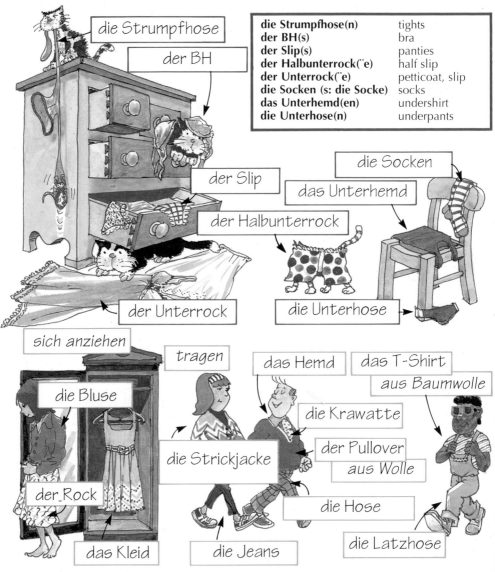

die Strumpfhose

der BH

die **Strumpfhose(n)**	tights
der **BH(s)**	bra
der **Slip(s)**	panties
der **Halbunterrock(˙e)**	half slip
der **Unterrock(˙e)**	petticoat, slip
die **Socken (s: die Socke)**	socks
das **Unterhemd(en)**	undershirt
die **Unterhose(n)**	underpants

die Socken

das Unterhemd

der Slip

der Halbunterrock

der Unterrock

die Unterhose

sich anziehen

tragen

das Hemd

das T-Shirt

aus Baumwolle

die Bluse

die Krawatte

die Strickjacke

der Pullover

aus Wolle

der Rock

die Hose

das Kleid

die Jeans

die Latzhose

sich anziehen	to get dressed		die **Krawatte(n)**	tie
die **Bluse(n)**	blouse		der **Pullover(-)**	sweater
der **Rock(˙e)**	skirt		**aus Wolle**	woollen
das **Kleid(er)**	dress		die **Hose(n)**	pants
tragen	to wear		das **T-Shirt(s)**	T-shirt
die **Strickjacke(n)**	cardigan		**aus Baumwolle**	cotton, made of
die **Jeans (pl)**	jeans			cotton
das **Hemd(en)**	shirt		die **Latzhose(n)**	dungarees

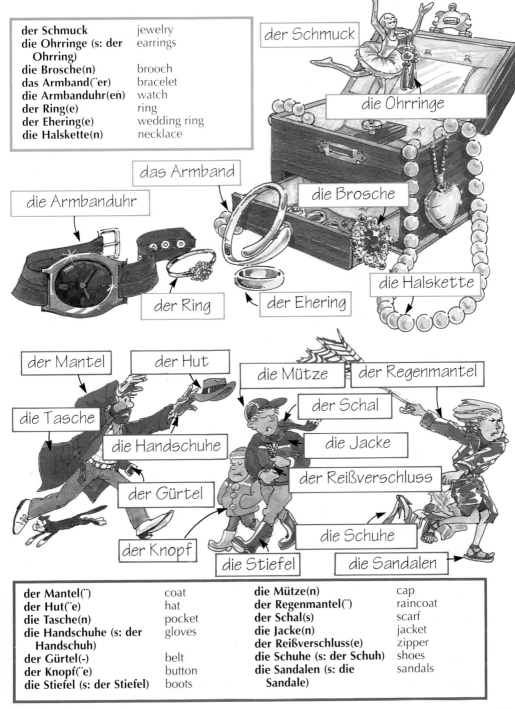

der Schmuck	jewelry
die Ohrringe (s: der Ohrring)	earrings
die Brosche(n)	brooch
das Armband(¨er)	bracelet
die Armbanduhr(en)	watch
der Ring(e)	ring
der Ehering(e)	wedding ring
die Halskette(n)	necklace

der Schmuck

die Ohrringe

das Armband

die Brosche

die Armbanduhr

die Halskette

der Ring

der Ehering

der Mantel

der Hut

die Mütze

der Regenmantel

die Tasche

der Schal

die Handschuhe

die Jacke

der Gürtel

der Reißverschluss

der Knopf

die Schuhe

die Stiefel

die Sandalen

German	English	German	English
der Mantel(¨)	coat	die Mütze(n)	cap
der Hut(¨e)	hat	der Regenmantel(¨)	raincoat
die Tasche(n)	pocket	der Schal(s)	scarf
die Handschuhe (s: der Handschuh)	gloves	die Jacke(n)	jacket
der Gürtel(-)	belt	der Reißverschluss(e)	zipper
der Knopf(¨e)	button	die Schuhe (s: der Schuh)	shoes
die Stiefel (s: der Stiefel)	boots	die Sandalen (s: die Sandale)	sandals

Going to bed

die Schlafenszeit	bedtime
das Licht anmachen	to switch the light on
schläfrig sein	to be sleepy
aufräumen	to tidy up
sich ausziehen	to get undressed

die Schlafenszeit

das Licht anmachen

schläfrig sein

aufräumen

sich ausziehen

das Badewasser einlaufen lassen

ein Bad nehmen

die Badewanne

der Stöpsel

der Bademantel

spritzen

die Badematte

die Waage

das Badewasser einlaufen lassen	to run a bath
ein Bad nehmen	to have a bath
die Badewanne(n)	bathtub
der Stöpsel(-)	plug
der Bademantel(¨)	bathrobe
spritzen	to splash
die Badematte(n)	bathmat
die Waage(n)	scales

24

ins Bett gehen

der Schlafanzug

das Nachthemd

die Hausschuhe

ins Bett gehen	to go to bed
der Schlafanzug(¨e)	pajamas
das Nachthemd(en)	nightgown
die Hausschuhe	slippers
(s: der Hausschuh)	

das Schlaflied

eine Geschichte vorlesen

das Kinderbett

einschlafen

das Schlaflied(er)	lullaby
eine Geschichte vorlesen	to read a story
das Kinderbett(en)	crib
einschlafen	to fall asleep

Gute Nacht.

Schlaf gut.

träumen

schlafen

schnarchen

das Kopfkissen

ausschalten

die Lampe

das Bettlaken

das Federbett

die Tagesdecke

der Nachttisch

das Bett

Gute Nacht.	Good-night.	**das Federbett(en)**	quilt
Schlaf gut.	Sleep well.	**das Bett(en)**	bed
träumen	to dream	**schnarchen**	to snore
schlafen	to sleep	**das Kopfkissen(-)**	pillow
ausschalten	to switch off	**das Bettlaken(-)**	sheet
die Lampe(n)	lamp	**die Tagesdecke(n)**	bedspread
der Nachttisch(e)	bedside table		

Eating and drinking

den Tisch decken	to lay the table
Das Essen ist fertig.	It's ready.
die Kaffeekanne(n)	coffee-pot
die Teekanne(n)	teapot
die Serviette(n)	napkin
das Glas(¨er)	glass
die Suppentasse(n)	bowl
der Teller(-)	plate
die Tasse(n)	cup
die Untertasse(n)	saucer
die Tischdecke(n)	tablecloth
der Krug(¨e)	pitcher
der Löffel(-)	spoon
das Messer(-)	knife
die Gabel(n)	fork

den Tisch decken

Das Essen ist fertig.

die Kaffeekanne

die Teekanne

die Serviette

der Löffel

das Messer

das Glas

die Tasse

die Untertasse

der Teller

die Gabel

der Krug

die Suppentasse

die Tischdecke

Greif zu.

Guten Appetit.

Hunger haben

Durst haben

essen

trinken

Das schmeckt gut.

gut gegessen haben

Greif zu.	Help yourself.
Guten Appetit.	Enjoy your meal.
Durst haben	to be thirsty
trinken	to drink
Hunger haben	to be hungry
essen	to eat
Das schmeckt gut.	It tastes good.
gut gegessen haben	to have eaten well

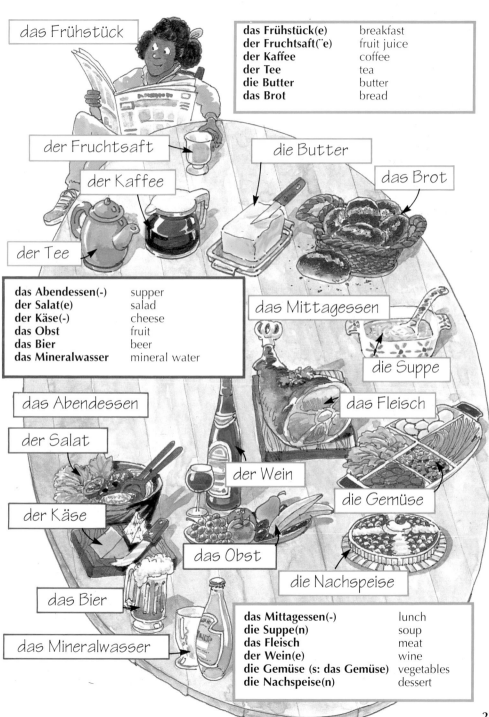

das Frühstück

das Frühstück(e)	breakfast
der Fruchtsaft(¨e)	fruit juice
der Kaffee	coffee
der Tee	tea
die Butter	butter
das Brot	bread

der Fruchtsaft

der Kaffee

die Butter

das Brot

der Tee

das Abendessen(-)	supper
der Salat(e)	salad
der Käse(-)	cheese
das Obst	fruit
das Bier	beer
das Mineralwasser	mineral water

das Mittagessen

die Suppe

das Abendessen

das Fleisch

der Salat

der Wein

die Gemüse

der Käse

das Obst

die Nachspeise

das Bier

das Mineralwasser

das Mittagessen(-)	lunch
die Suppe(n)	soup
das Fleisch	meat
der Wein(e)	wine
die Gemüse (s: das Gemüse)	vegetables
die Nachspeise(n)	dessert

Buying food

das Fleisch

die Leberwurst

die Salami

das Fleisch	meat
die Leberwurst(¨e)	liver sausage
die Salami(s)	salami
der Braten(-)	joint, roast
das Kotelett(s)	chop
das Huhn(¨er)	chicken
das Steak(s)	steak
der Schinken(-)	ham
das Kalbfleisch	veal
die Wurst(¨e)	sausage

der Braten

der Schinken

das Kalbfleisch

das Kotelett

das Steak

die Wurst

das Huhn

die Erbse

der Salat

das Gemüse

die Karotte

frisch

roh

der Spinat

die Tomate

der Weißkohl

der Knoblauch

der Blumenkohl

die Schnittbohne

die Zwiebel

der Rosenkohl

die Kartoffel

das Gemüse	vegetables	der Blumenkohl	cauliflower
frisch	fresh	der Rosenkohl	Brussels sprouts
der Weißkohl	cabbage	der Salat	salad
der Knoblauch	garlic	roh	raw
die Zwiebel(n)	onion	die Tomate(n)	tomato
die Erbse(n)	pea	die Schnittbohne(n)	green bean
die Karotte(n)	carrot	die Kartoffel(n)	potato
der Spinat	spinach		

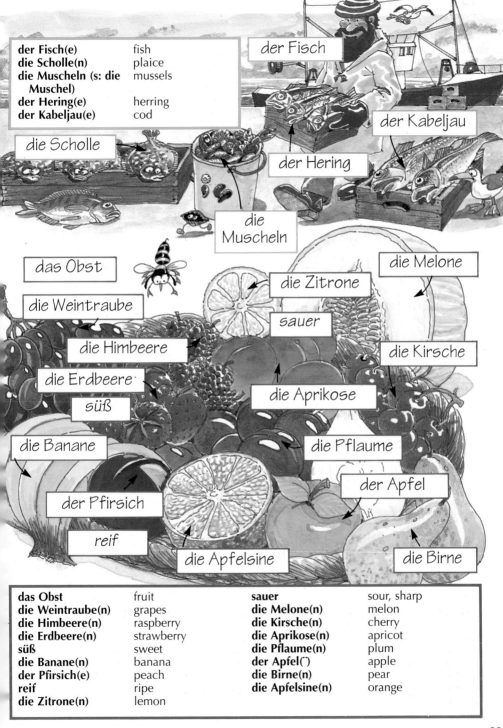

der Fisch(e)	fish
die Scholle(n)	plaice
die Muscheln (s: die Muschel)	mussels
der Hering(e)	herring
der Kabeljau(e)	cod

der Fisch

der Kabeljau

die Scholle

der Hering

die Muscheln

das Obst

die Melone

die Zitrone

die Weintraube

sauer

die Himbeere

die Kirsche

die Erdbeere

die Aprikose

süß

die Banane

die Pflaume

der Apfel

der Pfirsich

reif

die Apfelsine

die Birne

das Obst	fruit	**sauer**	sour, sharp
die Weintraube(n)	grapes	**die Melone(n)**	melon
die Himbeere(n)	raspberry	**die Kirsche(n)**	cherry
die Erdbeere(n)	strawberry	**die Aprikose(n)**	apricot
süß	sweet	**die Pflaume(n)**	plum
die Banane(n)	banana	**der Apfel(¨)**	apple
der Pfirsich(e)	peach	**die Birne(n)**	pear
reif	ripe	**die Apfelsine(n)**	orange
die Zitrone(n)	lemon		

Buying food

die Nudeln (pl)	noodles
die Linsen (pl)	lentils
die Bohnen (pl)	beans
die Sahne	cream
die Milch	milk
die Margarine	margarine
das Joghurt(s)	yogurt
der Honig	honey
die Eier (s: das Ei)	eggs
die Marmelade(n)	jam
der Zucker	sugar
das Mehl	flour

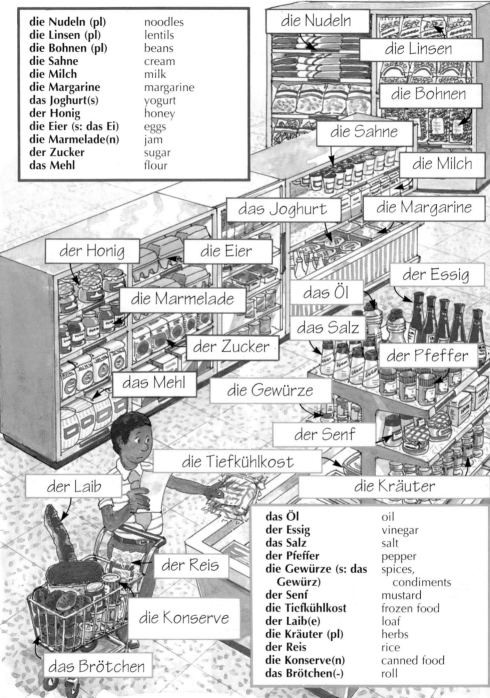

die Nudeln

die Linsen

die Bohnen

die Sahne

die Milch

das Joghurt

die Margarine

der Honig

die Eier

der Essig

die Marmelade

das Öl

das Salz

der Zucker

der Pfeffer

das Mehl

die Gewürze

der Senf

die Tiefkühlkost

die Kräuter

der Laib

der Reis

die Konserve

das Brötchen

das Öl	oil
der Essig	vinegar
das Salz	salt
der Pfeffer	pepper
die Gewürze (s: das Gewürz)	spices, condiments
der Senf	mustard
die Tiefkühlkost	frozen food
der Laib(e)	loaf
die Kräuter (pl)	herbs
der Reis	rice
die Konserve(n)	canned food
das Brötchen(-)	roll

die Schokolade	chocolate
der Keks(-)	cookie
das Obsttörtchen(-)	small tart
der Berliner Pfannkuchen(-)	doughnut
die Sahnetorte(n)	cream cake
das Eis	ice-cream
das Hefeteilchen(-)	Danish pastry

die Schokolade

der Keks

das Obsttörtchen

der Berliner Pfannkuchen

das Hefeteilchen

die Sahnetorte

das Eis

kochen

probieren

das Rezept

der Geschmack

die Zutat

rühren

Lecker!

kochen	to cook
das Rezept(e)	recipe
die Zutat(en)	ingredients
rühren	to mix
probieren	to taste
der Geschmack	flavor
Lecker!	Delicious!

Pastimes

fernsehen	to watch television
das Programm(e)	channel
die Sendung(en)	programme
Radio hören	to listen to the radio
die Kopfhörer (pl)	headphones
den Takt mitklopfen	to tap your feet

fernsehen

das Programm

die Sendung

Radio hören

die Kopfhörer

den Takt mitklopfen

Musik hören

der Kassetten-recorder

der Plattenspieler

die Kassette

die Platte

die Popmusik

die klassische Musik

Musik hören	to listen to music
der Kassetten-recorder(-)	cassette recorder
die Kassette(n)	cassette
der Plattenspieler(-)	record player
die Platte(n)	record
die Popmusik	pop music
die klassische Musik	classical music

lesen

die Heldin

die Zeitung

der Roman

der Held

die Zeitschrift

Gedichte

das Comic-Heft

lesen	to read
der Roman(e)	novel
die Heldin(nen)	heroine
der Held(en)	hero
die Zeitung(en)	newspaper
die Zeitschrift(en)	magazine
das Comic-Heft(e)	comic
Gedichte (s: das Gedicht)	poems, poetry

stricken

die Stricknadeln

das Muster

stricken	to knit
die Stricknadeln (pl)	knitting needles
das Muster(-)	pattern
die Wolle	yarn

die Wolle

nähen	to sew
der Stoff(e)	fabric
die Schere(n)	scissors
der Faden(ˉ)	thread
die Stecknadel(n)	pin
die Nadel(n)	needle
machen	to make

nähen

der Stoff

der Faden

machen

die Nadel

die Schere

die Stecknadel

das Tischlern

das Heimwerken

der Hammer

geschickt

reparieren

der Schraubenzieher

die Säge

bauen

das Tischlern	woodwork
das Heimwerken	odd jobs
die Säge(n)	saw
bauen	to make, to build
der Hammer(ˉ)	hammer
geschickt	skillful, good with your hands
reparieren	to mend
der Schraubenzieher(-)	screwdriver

Pastimes

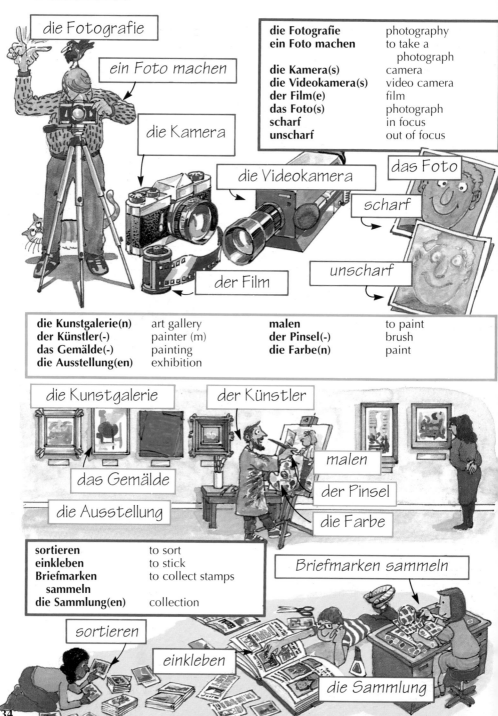

die Fotografie

ein Foto machen

die Kamera

die Fotografie	photography
ein Foto machen	to take a photograph
die Kamera(s)	camera
die Videokamera(s)	video camera
der Film(e)	film
das Foto(s)	photograph
scharf	in focus
unscharf	out of focus

die Videokamera

das Foto

scharf

unscharf

der Film

die Kunstgalerie(n)	art gallery	**malen**	to paint
der Künstler(-)	painter (m)	**der Pinsel(-)**	brush
das Gemälde(-)	painting	**die Farbe(n)**	paint
die Ausstellung(en)	exhibition		

die Kunstgalerie

der Künstler

das Gemälde

malen

die Ausstellung

der Pinsel

die Farbe

sortieren	to sort
einkleben	to stick
Briefmarken sammeln	to collect stamps
die Sammlung(en)	collection

Briefmarken sammeln

sortieren

einkleben

die Sammlung

die Musikerin(nen)	musician (f)	**Schlagzeug spielen**	to play the drums
das Instrument(e)	instrument	**Trompete spielen**	to play the trumpet
Geige spielen	to play the violin	**Cello spielen**	to play the cello
Klavier spielen	to play the piano	**das Orchester(-)**	orchestra
Gitarre spielen	to play the guitar	**der Dirigent(en)**	conductor (m)

die Musikerin

das Instrument

Geige spielen

Klavier spielen

Gitarre spielen

Schlagzeug spielen

Trompete spielen

Cello spielen

das Orchester

der Dirigent

singen

die Melodie

singen	to sing
die Melodie(n)	tune
der Chor(¨e)	choir
falsch singen	to sing out of tune

falsch singen

der Chor

die Spiele

die Spiele (s: das Spiel)	games
Karten spielen	to play cards
Dame spielen	to play draughts
Schach spielen	to play chess
das Brettspiel(e)	board game

Karten spielen

Dame spielen

das Brettspiel

Schach spielen

35

Going out

das Kino(s)	movie(s)
ins Kino gehen	to go to the movies
der Film(e)	film
der Platz(¨e)	seat
die Platzanweiserin(nen)	usherette
die Kasse(n)	box-office

das Kino

ins Kino gehen

der Film

die Platzanweiserin

die Kasse

der Platz

in die Disko gehen

der Diskjockey

in die Disko gehen	to go to a discothèque
der Diskjockey(s)	disc jockey
tanzen	to dance
die Tanzfläche(n)	dance floor

tanzen

die Tanzfläche

das Theater

das Stück

das Bühnenbild

Zugabe!

die Schauspielerin

der Scheinwerfer

der Schauspieler

die Bühne

das Publikum

das Theater(-)	theatre
das Stück(e)	play
das Bühnenbild(er)	scenery
der Scheinwerfer(-)	spotlight
die Schauspielerin(nen)	actress
der Schauspieler(-)	actor
die Bühne(n)	stage
das Publikum	audience
klatschen	to clap
sich gut unterhalten	to enjoy yourself
Zugabe!	Encore!

klatschen

sich gut unterhalten

das Ballett

auftreten

der Balletttänzer

die Oper

der Sänger

berühmt

das Ballett	ballet	**die Oper(n)**	opera
der Balletttänzer(-)	ballet dancer (m)	**der Sänger(-)**	singer (m)
auftreten	to perform, to appear on stage	**berühmt**	famous

das Restaurant

der Ober

Ohne Bedienung!

die Speisekarte

Mit Bedienung?

die Rechnung

Was hätten Sie gerne?

bestellen

servieren

das Trinkgeld

das Tablett

die Vorspeise

das Hauptgericht

das Dessert

das Restaurant(s)	restaurant	**das Dessert(s)**	dessert, pudding
der Ober(-)	waiter	**die Rechnung(en)**	bill
die Speisekarte(n)	menu	**Mit Bedienung?**	Is service included?
Was hätten Sie gerne?	What would you like?	**Ohne Bedienung!**	Service not included!
bestellen	to order		
servieren	to serve	**das Trinkgeld(er)**	tip
die Vorspeise(n)	starter	**das Tablett(s)**	tray
das Hauptgericht(e)	main course		

At the zoo

der Zoo(s)	zoo
das Tier(e)	animal
das Zebra(s)	zebra
die Giraffe(n)	giraffe
der Eisbär(en)	polar bear
der Elefant(en)	elephant
der Rüssel(-)	trunk
der Stoßzahn(¨e)	tusk
der Gorilla(s)	gorilla
wild	wild
zahm	tame
füttern	to feed
der Wärter(-)	keeper (m)

der Zoo

das Tier

das Zebra

die Giraffe

der Eisbär

der Rüssel

der Elefant

der Gorilla

füttern

wild

zahm

der Stoßzahn

der Wärter

In the park

der Park(s)	park
der Teich(e)	pond
das Ruderboot(e)	rowing boat
rudern	to row
das Ruder(-)	oar
das Picknick(e)	picnic
die Bank(¨e)	bench
sich ausruhen	to rest

der Park

der Teich

das Ruder

das Ruderboot

rudern

sich ausruhen

das Picknick

die Bank

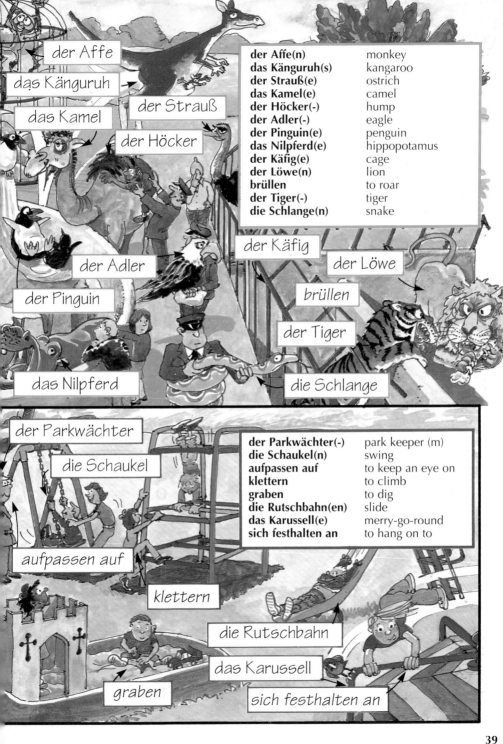

der Affe

das Känguruh

das Kamel

der Strauß

der Höcker

der Affe(n)	monkey
das Känguruh(s)	kangaroo
der Strauß(e)	ostrich
das Kamel(e)	camel
der Höcker(-)	hump
der Adler(-)	eagle
der Pinguin(e)	penguin
das Nilpferd(e)	hippopotamus
der Käfig(e)	cage
der Löwe(n)	lion
brüllen	to roar
der Tiger(-)	tiger
die Schlange(n)	snake

der Käfig

der Adler

der Löwe

der Pinguin

brüllen

der Tiger

das Nilpferd

die Schlange

der Parkwächter

die Schaukel

der Parkwächter(-)	park keeper (m)
die Schaukel(n)	swing
aufpassen auf	to keep an eye on
klettern	to climb
graben	to dig
die Rutschbahn(en)	slide
das Karussell(e)	merry-go-round
sich festhalten an	to hang on to

aufpassen auf

klettern

die Rutschbahn

das Karussell

graben

sich festhalten an

39

In the city

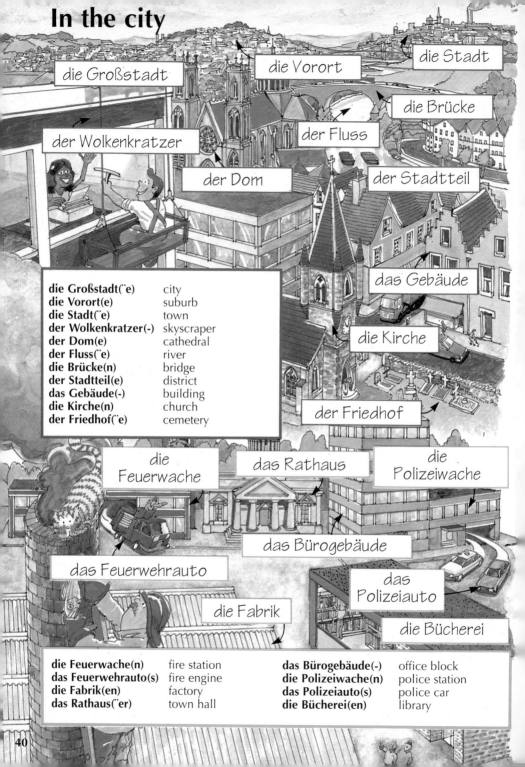

die Stadt

die Vorort

die Großstadt

die Brücke

der Wolkenkratzer

der Fluss

der Dom

der Stadtteil

das Gebäude

die Kirche

der Friedhof

die Großstadt(¨e)	city
die Vorort(e)	suburb
die Stadt(¨e)	town
der Wolkenkratzer(-)	skyscraper
der Dom(e)	cathedral
der Fluss(¨e)	river
die Brücke(n)	bridge
der Stadtteil(e)	district
das Gebäude(-)	building
die Kirche(n)	church
der Friedhof(¨e)	cemetery

die Feuerwache

das Rathaus

die Polizeiwache

das Bürogebäude

das Feuerwehrauto

das Polizeiauto

die Fabrik

die Bücherei

die Feuerwache(n)	fire station	**das Bürogebäude(-)**	office block
das Feuerwehrauto(s)	fire engine	**die Polizeiwache(n)**	police station
die Fabrik(en)	factory	**das Polizeiauto(s)**	police car
das Rathaus(¨er)	town hall	**die Bücherei(en)**	library

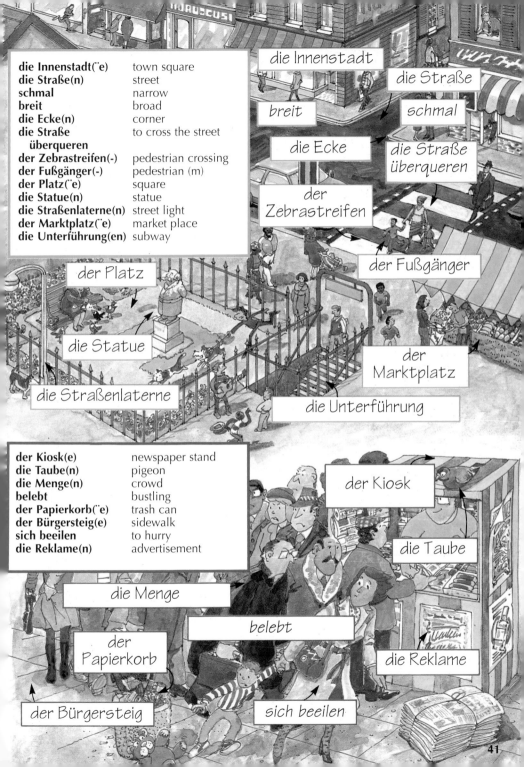

die Innenstadt(¨e)	town square
die Straße(n)	street
schmal	narrow
breit	broad
die Ecke(n)	corner
die Straße überqueren	to cross the street
der Zebrastreifen(-)	pedestrian crossing
der Fußgänger(-)	pedestrian (m)
der Platz(¨e)	square
die Statue(n)	statue
die Straßenlaterne(n)	street light
der Marktplatz(¨e)	market place
die Unterführung(en)	subway

die Innenstadt

die Straße

breit

schmal

die Ecke

die Straße überqueren

der Zebrastreifen

der Fußgänger

der Platz

die Statue

die Straßenlaterne

der Marktplatz

die Unterführung

der Kiosk(e)	newspaper stand
die Taube(n)	pigeon
die Menge(n)	crowd
belebt	bustling
der Papierkorb(¨e)	trash can
der Bürgersteig(e)	sidewalk
sich beeilen	to hurry
die Reklame(n)	advertisement

der Kiosk

die Taube

die Menge

belebt

die Reklame

der Papierkorb

der Bürgersteig

sich beeilen

41

Shopping

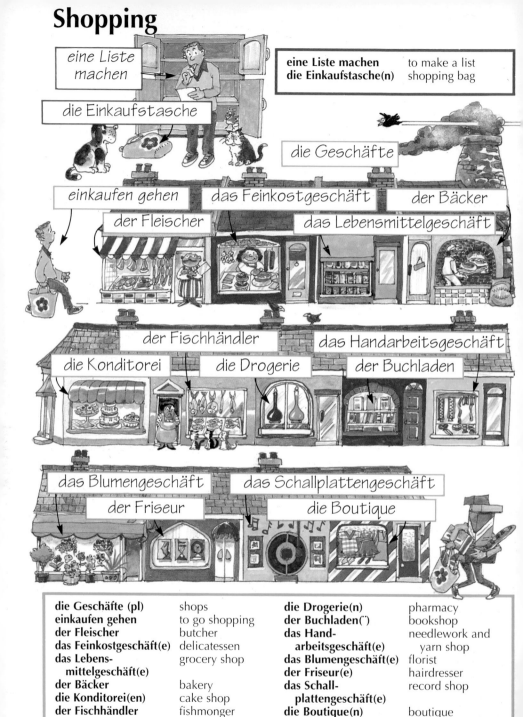

eine Liste machen

eine Liste machen — to make a list
die Einkaufstasche(n) — shopping bag

die Einkaufstasche

die Geschäfte

einkaufen gehen

das Feinkostgeschäft

der Bäcker

der Fleischer

das Lebensmittelgeschäft

der Fischhändler

das Handarbeitsgeschäft

die Konditorei

die Drogerie

der Buchladen

das Blumengeschäft

das Schallplattengeschäft

der Friseur

die Boutique

die Geschäfte (pl)	shops	die Drogerie(n)	pharmacy
einkaufen gehen	to go shopping	der Buchladen(¨)	bookshop
der Fleischer	butcher	das Hand-	needlework and
das Feinkostgeschäft(e)	delicatessen	arbeitsgeschäft(e)	yarn shop
das Lebens-	grocery shop	das Blumengeschäft(e)	florist
mittelgeschäft(e)		der Friseur(e)	hairdresser
der Bäcker	bakery	das Schall-	record shop
die Konditorei(en)	cake shop	plattengeschäft(e)	
der Fischhändler	fishmonger	die Boutique(n)	boutique

auf dem Markt einkaufen

der Marktstand

anstehen

Das macht...

Wie viel macht das?

wiegen

Ein Kilo...

Ein Pfund...

auf dem Markt einkaufen	to shop at the market
der Marktstand(˙e)	stall
anstehen	to line up

Wie viel macht das?	How much is that?
Das macht...	That will be...
wiegen	to weigh
Ein Kilo...	A kilo of...
Ein Pfund...	Half a kilo of...

in den Supermarkt gehen

der Lautsprecher

der Einkaufskorb

die Theke

der Gang

die Dose

das Päckchen

der Einkaufswagen

die Flasche

der Eingang

der Ausgang

die Kasse

die Tragetasche

die Kassiererin

in den Supermarkt gehen	to go to the supermarket
der Einkaufskorb(˙e)	basket
der Einkaufswagen(-)	shopping cart
der Lautsprecher(-)	loudspeaker
die Theke(n)	counter
der Gang(˙e)	aisle
die Dose(n)	can
das Päckchen(-)	packet
die Flasche(n)	bottle
der Eingang(˙e)	entrance
der Ausgang(˙e)	exit
die Kasse(n)	checkout
die Tragetasche(n)	bag
die Kassiererin(nen)	cashier (f)

43

Shopping

einen Schaufenster-bummel machen	to go window-shopping	**das Sonderangebot(e)**	bargain
das Schaufenster(-)	shop window	**die Kundin(nen)**	customer (f)
Das ist preiswert.	It's good value.	**kaufen**	to buy
Das ist teuer.	It's expensive.	**die Verkäuferin(nen)**	shop assistant (f)
SCHLUSSVERKAUF (m)	sale	**verkaufen**	to sell

Geld ausgeben	to spend money	**Welche Größe ist es?**	What size is this?
der Preis(e)	price	**klein**	small
die Quittung(en)	receipt	**mittel**	medium
Womit kann ich dienen?	Can I help you?	**groß**	large
		Was kostet…?	How much is…?
Ich hätte gern…	I'd like…	**Das kostet…**	It costs…

der Buchladen(¨) und die Schreibwarenhandlung(en)	bookshop and stationer's	**die Postkarte(n)**	postcard
das Buch(¨er)	book	**der Kuli(s)**	ball-point pen
das Taschenbuch(¨er)	paperback	**der Bleistift(e)**	pencil
der Umschlag(¨e)	envelope	**das Schreibpapier**	writing paper

der Buchladen und die Schreibwarenhandlung

der Umschlag

die Postkarte

das Buch

der Kuli

der Bleistift

das Taschenbuch

das Schreibpapier

das Kaufhaus

die Abteilung

der Aufzug

die Rolltreppe

Spielwaren

Sportabteilung

Möbel

Oberbekleidung

das Kaufhaus(¨er)	department store	**Spielwaren (pl)**	Toys
die Abteilung(en)	department	**Möbel (pl)**	Furniture
die Rolltreppe(n)	escalator	**Sportabteilung (f)**	Sports equipment
der Aufzug(¨e)	elevator	**Oberbekleidung (f)**	Clothes

At the post office and bank

das Postamt(¨er)	post office	**schicken**	to send
der Briefkasten(¨)	mail-box	**das Telegramm(e)**	telegram
einwerfen	to mail	**das Formular(e)**	form
der Brief(e)	letter	**die Briefmarke(n)**	stamp
das Paket(e)	package	**Luftpost**	airmail
die Leerung(en)	collection,	**die Adresse(n)**	address
	collection time	**die Postleitzahl(en)**	zip code

das Postamt

schicken

das Telegramm

der Briefkasten

einwerfen

das Formular

der Brief

das Paket

die Leerung

die Briefmarke

Luftpost

die Adresse

der Briefträger

die Postleitzahl

die Post

austeilen

der Briefträger(-)	postman (m)
die Post	mail
austeilen	to deliver

die Bank

der Kassierer

das Geld

Haben Sie Kleingeld?

Geld wechseln

die Münze

der Umtauschkurs

der Geschäftsführer der Bank

die Banknote

die Kreditkarte

Geld einzahlen

Geld abheben

die Brieftasche

das Scheckbuch

einen Scheck ausstellen

die Geldbörse

die Handtasche

die Bank(en)	bank	**die Banknote(n)**	paper money
das Geld	money	**die Kreditkarte(n)**	credit card
Geld wechseln	to change money	**Geld einzahlen**	to put money in
der Umtauschkurs(e)	exchange rate	**Geld abheben**	to take money out
der Geschäftsführer(-)	bank manager	**das Scheckbuch(¨er)**	check-book
der Bank		**einen Scheck**	to write a check
der Kassierer(-)	cashier (m)	**ausstellen**	
Haben Sie Kleingeld?	Have you any small change?	**die Brieftasche(n)**	wallet
		die Geldbörse(n)	purse
die Münze(n)	coin	**die Handtasche(n)**	handbag

47

Phonecalls and letters

telefonieren	to make a phonecall	das Telefonbuch(¨er)	telephone directory
		läuten	to ring
das Telefon(e)	telephone	ans Telefon gehen	to answer the phone
der Telefonhörer(-)	receiver		
den Telefonhörer abnehmen	to pick up the receiver	Hier ist Anke.	It's Anke.
		Ich rufe dich zurück.	I'll call you back.
wählen	to dial	Wiederhören	Goodbye
die Telefonnummer(n)	telephone number	auflegen	to hang up
die Vorwahl	area code		

die Telefonzelle(n)	telephone box
der Notfall(¨e)	emergency
der Notruf	911 call

* When speaking German, the most usual way of answering the phone is to say your name.

einen Brief schreiben

25 . 10 . 02

Sehr geehrte Damen und Herren,

Vielen Dank für Ihren Brief vom...

Beigefügt finden Sie...

...postwendend.

Mit freundlichen Grüßen...

einen Brief schreiben	to write a letter	**Beigefügt finden Sie...**	I enclose…
Sehr geehrte Damen und Herren,	Dear Sir/Madam,	**postwendend**	by return mail
Vielen Dank für Ihren Brief vom...	Thank you for your letter of…	**Mit freundlichen Grüßen...**	Yours faithfully,

einen Brief öffnen

Liebe Anke,

Schön, mal wieder von dir zu hören. Mit getrennter Post erhältst du...

9 . 1 . 2002

Alles Gute...

einen Brief öffnen	to open a letter	**Mit getrennter Post erhältst du...**	I am sending… separately.
Liebe Anke,	Dear Anke,	**Alles Gute...**	Love from…
Schön, mal wieder von dir zu hören.	It was lovely to hear from you.		

eine Ansichtskarte schicken

ein Telegramm schicken

Es ist ganz toll hier. Schade, dass du nicht hier bist.

Dringend stop sofort zu Hause anrufen stop

eine Ansichtskarte schicken	to send a postcard	**ein Telegramm schicken**	to send a telegram
Es ist ganz toll hier.	Having a lovely time.	**Dringend stop sofort zu Hause anrufen stop**	Urgent message stop phone home stop
Schade, dass du nicht hier bist.	Wish you were here.		

Out and about

gehen

laufen

In welcher Richtung ist...?

das Hinweisschild

nach dem Weg fragen

die Karte

Wie weit ist...?

der Sportwagen

gehen	to walk	nach dem Weg fragen	to ask the way
laufen	to run	die Karte(n)	map
der Sportwagen(-)	stroller	das Hinweisschild(er)	signpost
In welcher Richtung ist...?	Which way is...?	Wie weit ist...?	How far is...?

mit dem Bus fahren

der Passagier

aussteigen

die Fahrkarte

die U-Bahnstation

einsteigen

der Bus

die U-Bahn

die Bushaltestelle

mit dem Bus fahren	to take the bus	der Bus(se)	bus
der Passagier(e)	passenger (m/f)	die Bushaltestelle(n)	bus stop
aussteigen	to get off	die U-Bahnstation(en)	subway station
einsteigen	to get on		
die Fahrkarte(n)	ticket	die U-Bahn(en)	subway

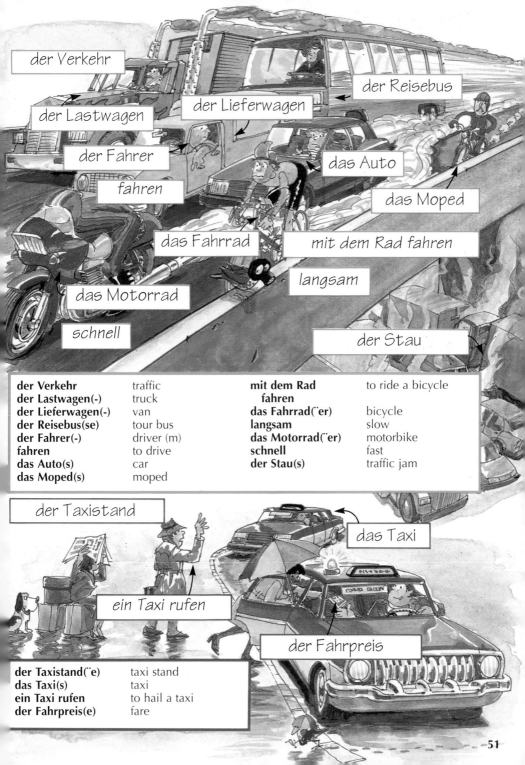

der Verkehr

der Reisebus

der Lieferwagen

der Lastwagen

der Fahrer

das Auto

fahren

das Moped

das Fahrrad

mit dem Rad fahren

langsam

das Motorrad

schnell

der Stau

der Verkehr	traffic	mit dem Rad fahren	to ride a bicycle
der Lastwagen(-)	truck	das Fahrrad(¨er)	bicycle
der Lieferwagen(¨)	van	langsam	slow
der Reisebus(se)	tour bus	das Motorrad(¨er)	motorbike
der Fahrer(-)	driver (m)	schnell	fast
fahren	to drive	der Stau(s)	traffic jam
das Auto(s)	car		
das Moped(s)	moped		

der Taxistand

das Taxi

ein Taxi rufen

der Fahrpreis

der Taxistand(¨e)	taxi stand
das Taxi(s)	taxi
ein Taxi rufen	to hail a taxi
der Fahrpreis(e)	fare

Driving

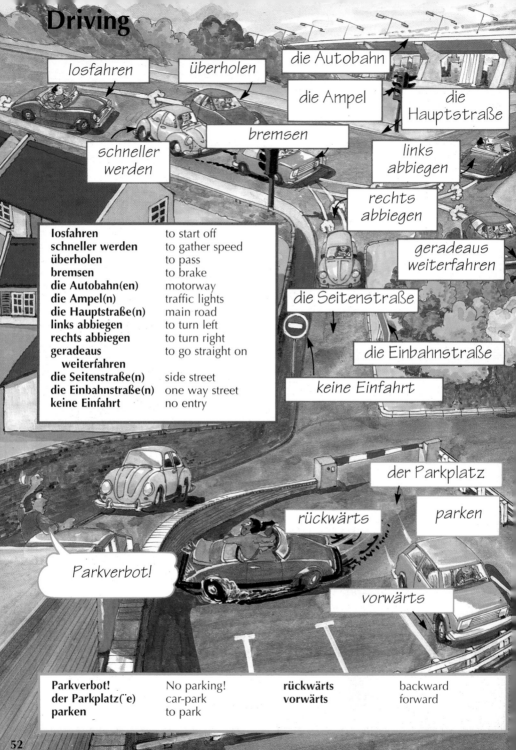

losfahren

überholen

die Autobahn

die Ampel

die Hauptstraße

bremsen

schneller werden

links abbiegen

rechts abbiegen

geradeaus weiterfahren

die Seitenstraße

die Einbahnstraße

keine Einfahrt

losfahren	to start off
schneller werden	to gather speed
überholen	to pass
bremsen	to brake
die Autobahn(en)	motorway
die Ampel(n)	traffic lights
die Hauptstraße(n)	main road
links abbiegen	to turn left
rechts abbiegen	to turn right
geradeaus weiterfahren	to go straight on
die Seitenstraße(n)	side street
die Einbahnstraße(n)	one way street
keine Einfahrt	no entry

der Parkplatz

rückwärts

parken

Parkverbot!

vorwärts

Parkverbot!	No parking!	**rückwärts**	backward
der Parkplatz(¨e)	car-park	**vorwärts**	forward
parken	to park		

der Unfall(¨e)	accident
das Lenkrad(¨er)	steering wheel
die Windschutzscheibe(n)	windshield
der Sicherheitsgurt(e)	safety belt
der Blinker(-)	indicator
der Scheinwerfer(-)	headlight
die Motorhaube(n)	hood
der Kofferraum(¨e)	trunk
das Nummernschild(er)	license plate
das Rad(¨er)	wheel
der Reifen(-)	tire
die Hupe(n)	horn

der Unfall

das Lenkrad

die Windschutzscheibe

der Blinker

der Sicherheitsgurt

der Scheinwerfer

die Motorhaube

der Kofferraum

das Nummernschild

das Rad

einen Platten haben

der Reifen

eine Panne haben

die Hupe

das Öl

der Automechaniker

die Tankstelle

volltanken

das Benzin

einen Platten haben	to have a flat tire
eine Panne haben	to have a breakdown
der Automechaniker(-)	mechanic (m)
das Öl	oil
die Tankstelle(n)	gas station
volltanken	to fill up with gas
das Benzin	gas

Traveling by train

der Bahnhof

die Gepäckaufbewahrung

der Gepäckträger

der Kontrolleur

der Wartesaal

die Schranke

der Reisende

der Fahrplan

Der Zug nach…

Der Zug aus…

der Fahrkartenschalter

die Fahrkarte

die Rückfahrkarte

die Zeitkarte

der Fahrkartenautomat

einen Platz reservieren

die Bahnsteigkarte

der Bahnhof("e)	station	Der Zug aus…	The train from…
der Gepäckträger(-)	porter (m)	der Fahrkarten-	ticket office
die Gepäckauf-	left luggage office	schalter(-)	
bewahrung		die Fahrkarte(n)	ticket
der Kontrolleur(e)	ticket collector (m)	die Rückfahrkarte(n)	return ticket
der Wartesaal	waiting-room	die Zeitkarte(n)	season ticket
(die Wartesäle)		der Fahrkarten-	ticket machine
die Schranke(n)	barrier	automat(en)	
der Reisende(n)	traveler (m)	die Bahnsteigkarte(n)	platform ticket
der Fahrplan("e)	timetable	einen Platz	to reserve a seat
Der Zug nach…	The train to…	reservieren	

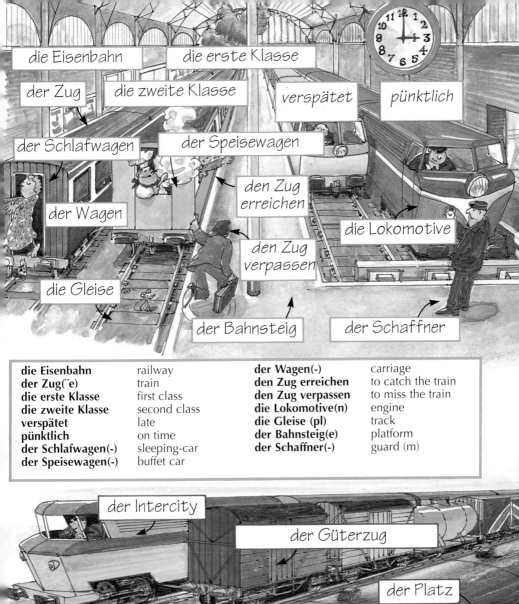

die Eisenbahn

die erste Klasse

der Zug

die zweite Klasse

verspätet

pünktlich

der Schlafwagen

der Speisewagen

den Zug erreichen

der Wagen

die Lokomotive

den Zug verpassen

die Gleise

der Bahnsteig

der Schaffner

die Eisenbahn	railway	**der Wagen(-)**	carriage
der Zug(¨e)	train	**den Zug erreichen**	to catch the train
die erste Klasse	first class	**den Zug verpassen**	to miss the train
die zweite Klasse	second class	**die Lokomotive(n)**	engine
verspätet	late	**die Gleise (pl)**	track
pünktlich	on time	**der Bahnsteig(e)**	platform
der Schlafwagen(-)	sleeping-car	**der Schaffner(-)**	guard (m)
der Speisewagen(-)	buffet car		

der Intercity

der Güterzug

der Platz

der reservierte Platz

die Gepäckablage

Nichtrauche

der Intercity	inter-city train
der Güterzug(¨e)	freight train
der Platz(¨e)	seat
der reservierte Platz	reserved seat
die Gepäckablage(n)	luggage-rack
Nichtraucher	No smoking

55

Traveling by plane and boat

der Flughafen

das Flugzeug

Ankunft

fliegen

die Landebahn

landen

starten

der Zoll

der Zollbeamte

Nichts zu verzollen.

der Pass

der Flughafen(¨)	airport
das Flugzeug(e)	airplane
fliegen	to fly
Ankunft (f)	Arrivals
die Landebahn(en)	runway
landen	to land
starten	to take off

der Zoll	customs
der Zollbeamte(n)	customs officer (m)
Nichts zu verzollen.	Nothing to declare.
der Pass(¨e)	passport

der Hafen

mit dem Schiff fahren

das Schiff

das Passagierschiff

der Schornstein

die Flagge

die Kabine

der Kapitän

das Bullauge

das Deck

der Anker

die Landungsbrücke

der Hafen(¨)	port		**der Anker(-)**	anchor
mit dem Schiff fahren	to travel by boat, to sail		**die Kabine(n)**	cabin
			das Deck(s)	deck
das Schiff(e)	ship		**der Schornstein(e)**	smoke stack
das Passagierschiff(e)	liner		**der Kapitän(e)**	captain
die Flagge(n)	flag		**die Landungsbrücke(n)**	gangway
das Bullauge(n)	porthole			

Abflug (m)	Departures
der Duty-free-Shop	duty-free shop
der Check-in	check-in
der Flugschein(e)	airline ticket
der Anhänger(-)	label
der Gepäckwagen(-)	luggage cart
Bitte anschnallen.	Fasten your seatbelts.
der Pilot(en)	pilot
die Besatzung(en)	crew
die Stewardess(en)	stewardess
einsteigen	to board
der Koffer(-)	suitcase
das Handgepäck	hand luggage

Abflug

der Duty-free-Shop

Bitte anschnallen.

der Pilot

die Besatzung

der Check-in

die Stewardess

der Koffer

einsteigen

der Flugschein

der Anhänger

der Gepäckwagen

das Handgepäck

die Fähre

der Kai

die Überfahrt

seekrank sein

die Ladung

laden

ausladen

der Laderaum

der Seemann

die Fähre(n)	ferry
die Überfahrt(en)	crossing
seekrank sein	to be seasick
der Kai(s)	docks, quay
die Ladung(en)	cargo
laden	to load
ausladen	to unload
der Laderaum(¨e)	hold
der Seemann (die Seeleute)	sailor

On vacation

in Urlaub fahren

packen

die Touristin

in Urlaub fahren	to go on vacation
packen	to pack
das Sonnenschutz-mittel(-)	suntan lotion
die Sonnenbrille(n)	sunglasses
die Touristin(nen)	tourist (f)
etwas besichtigen	to sightsee

das Sonnenschutzmittel

die Sonnenbrille

etwas besichtigen

im Hotel wohnen

das Hotel

der Empfang

der Portier

mit Dusche

das Einzelzimmer

mit Balkon

das Doppelzimmer

ein Zimmer reservieren

die Pension

belegt

das Hotel(s)	hotel	**belegt**	fully booked
im Hotel wohnen	to stay in a hotel	**ein Zimmer reservieren**	to reserve a room
der Empfang	reception		
der Portier(s)	porter	**mit Dusche**	with shower
das Einzelzimmer(-)	single room	**mit Balkon**	with balcony
das Doppelzimmer(-)	double room	**die Pension**	guest house

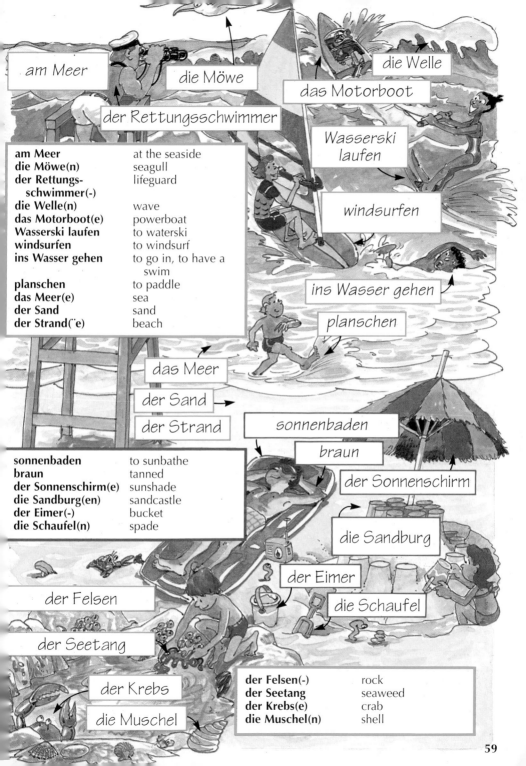

am Meer

die Möwe

die Welle

das Motorboot

der Rettungsschwimmer

Wasserski laufen

windsurfen

am Meer	at the seaside
die Möwe(n)	seagull
der Rettungs-	lifeguard
schwimmer(-)	
die Welle(n)	wave
das Motorboot(e)	powerboat
Wasserski laufen	to waterski
windsurfen	to windsurf
ins Wasser gehen	to go in, to have a swim
planschen	to paddle
das Meer(e)	sea
der Sand	sand
der Strand(¨e)	beach

ins Wasser gehen

planschen

das Meer

der Sand

der Strand

sonnenbaden

braun

der Sonnenschirm

sonnenbaden	to sunbathe
braun	tanned
der Sonnenschirm(e)	sunshade
die Sandburg(en)	sandcastle
der Eimer(-)	bucket
die Schaufel(n)	spade

die Sandburg

der Eimer

die Schaufel

der Felsen

der Seetang

der Krebs

die Muschel

der Felsen(-)	rock
der Seetang	seaweed
der Krebs(e)	crab
die Muschel(n)	shell

On vacation

zum Bergsteigen gehen	to go mountaineering
der Berg(e)	mountain
der Gipfel(-)	summit
die Aussicht	view
steil	steep
klettern	to climb
der Bergsteiger(-)	climber (m)
der Rucksack(¨e)	rucksack, backpack

zum Skilaufen gehen

der Skiort

zum Bergsteigen gehen

der Gipfel

der Sessellift

der Berg

die Aussicht

klettern

steil

der Bergsteiger

der Skilehrer

der Rucksack

der Hang

der Schlitten

der Skistock

die Skistiefel

die Skier

zum Skilaufen gehen	to go skiing
der Skiort(e)	ski resort
der Sessellift(e)	chairlift
der Skilehrer(-)	ski instructor (m)
der Hang(¨e)	ski slope, ski run
der Schlitten(-)	sledge
der Skistock(¨e)	ski pole
die Skistiefel (pl)	ski boots
die Skier (pl)	skis

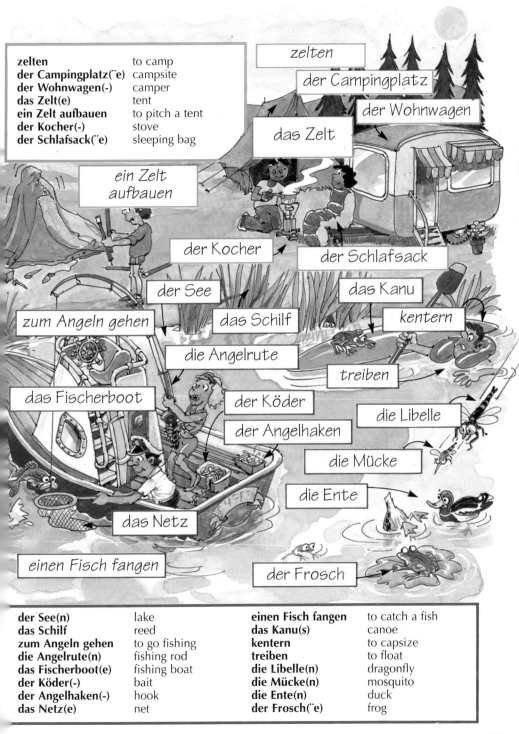

zelten	to camp
der Campingplatz(¨e)	campsite
der Wohnwagen(-)	camper
das Zelt(e)	tent
ein Zelt aufbauen	to pitch a tent
der Kocher(-)	stove
der Schlafsack(¨e)	sleeping bag

zelten

der Campingplatz

der Wohnwagen

das Zelt

ein Zelt aufbauen

der Kocher

der Schlafsack

der See

das Kanu

zum Angeln gehen

das Schilf

kentern

die Angelrute

treiben

das Fischerboot

der Köder

die Libelle

der Angelhaken

die Mücke

die Ente

das Netz

einen Fisch fangen

der Frosch

der See(n)	lake	**einen Fisch fangen**	to catch a fish
das Schilf	reed	**das Kanu(s)**	canoe
zum Angeln gehen	to go fishing	**kentern**	to capsize
die Angelrute(n)	fishing rod	**treiben**	to float
das Fischerboot(e)	fishing boat	**die Libelle(n)**	dragonfly
der Köder(-)	bait	**die Mücke(n)**	mosquito
der Angelhaken(-)	hook	**die Ente(n)**	duck
das Netz(e)	net	**der Frosch(¨e)**	frog

In the countryside

das Dorf

die Landschaft

friedlich

das Land

das Bauernhaus

spazieren gehen

der Pfad

die Wiese

der Bach

das Kaninchen

der Maulwurf

auf einen Baum klettern

die Wiesenblumen

Blumen pflücken

der Blumenstrauß

das Gänseblümchen

die Butterblume

das Dorf("er)	village
die Landschaft(en)	landscape
friedlich	peaceful
das Land	countryside
das Bauernhaus("er)	farmhouse
spazieren gehen	to go for a walk

der Pfad(e)	path
der Bach("e)	stream
die Wiese(n)	meadow
das Kaninchen(-)	rabbit
der Maulwurf("e)	mole
auf einen Baum klettern	to climb a tree
die Wiesenblumen (pl)	wild flowers
Blumen pflücken	to pick flowers
der Blumenstrauß("e)	bunch of flowers
das Gänseblümchen(-)	daisy
die Butterblume(n)	buttercup

der Wald

die Eiche

die Tanne

das Blatt

der Ast

die Eule

die Amsel

das Eichhörnchen

der Wald(ˮer)	wood
die Eiche(n)	oak tree
die Tanne(n)	pine tree
das Blatt(ˮer)	leaf
der Ast(ˮe)	branch
die Eule(n)	owl
die Amsel(n)	blackbird
das Eichhörnchen(-)	squirrel
die Drossel(n)	thrush
der Fuchs(ˮe)	fox
fliegen	to fly
der Spatz(en)	sparrow

fliegen

der Spatz

die Drossel

der Fuchs

das Tal(ˮer)	valley
der Hügel(-)	hill
die Brücke(n)	bridge
der Hang(ˮe)	slope
die Trauerweide(n)	weeping willow
das Ufer(-)	bank
der Fluss(ˮe)	river
die Fliege(n)	fly
die Spinne(n)	spider
die Mücke(n)	mosquito

das Tal

der Hügel

die Brücke

der Hang

die Trauerweide

das Ufer

der Fluss

die Spinne

die Fliege

die Mücke

63

On the farm

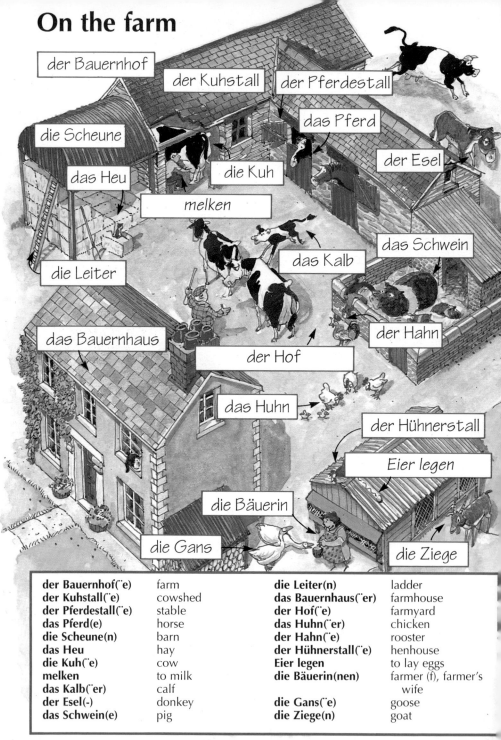

der Bauernhof

der Kuhstall

der Pferdestall

das Pferd

die Scheune

der Esel

das Heu

die Kuh

melken

das Schwein

die Leiter

das Kalb

das Bauernhaus

der Hahn

der Hof

das Huhn

der Hühnerstall

Eier legen

die Bäuerin

die Gans

die Ziege

der Bauernhof(¨e)	farm	**die Leiter(n)**	ladder
der Kuhstall(¨e)	cowshed	**das Bauernhaus(¨er)**	farmhouse
der Pferdestall(¨e)	stable	**der Hof(¨e)**	farmyard
das Pferd(e)	horse	**das Huhn(¨er)**	chicken
die Scheune(n)	barn	**der Hahn(¨e)**	rooster
das Heu	hay	**der Hühnerstall(¨e)**	henhouse
die Kuh(¨e)	cow	**Eier legen**	to lay eggs
melken	to milk	**die Bäuerin(nen)**	farmer (f), farmer's
das Kalb(¨er)	calf		wife
der Esel(-)	donkey	**die Gans(¨e)**	goose
das Schwein(e)	pig	**die Ziege(n)**	goat

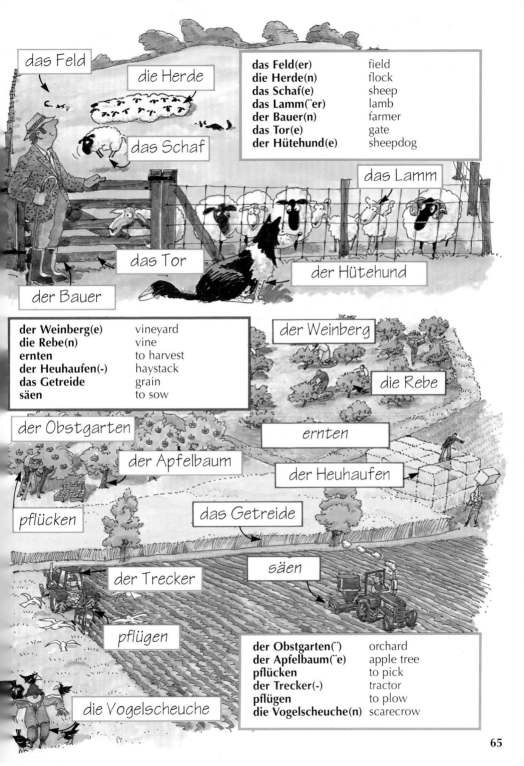

das Feld

die Herde

das Feld(er)	field
die Herde(n)	flock
das Schaf(e)	sheep
das Lamm(¨er)	lamb
der Bauer(n)	farmer
das Tor(e)	gate
der Hütehund(e)	sheepdog

das Schaf

das Lamm

das Tor

der Hütehund

der Bauer

der Weinberg(e)	vineyard
die Rebe(n)	vine
ernten	to harvest
der Heuhaufen(-)	haystack
das Getreide	grain
säen	to sow

der Weinberg

die Rebe

der Obstgarten

ernten

der Apfelbaum

der Heuhaufen

pflücken

das Getreide

der Trecker

säen

pflügen

der Obstgarten(¨)	orchard
der Apfelbaum(¨e)	apple tree
pflücken	to pick
der Trecker(-)	tractor
pflügen	to plow
die Vogelscheuche(n)	scarecrow

die Vogelscheuche

65

At work

zu spät kommen

die Mittagspause

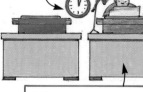

zur Arbeit gehen

pünktlich sein

Überstunden

zur Arbeit gehen	to go to work	**die Mittagspause(n)**	lunch hour
zu spät kommen	to be late	**Überstunden (pl)**	overtime
pünktlich sein	to be on time		

das Büro

jemanden einstellen

fleißig

aufhören zu arbeiten

die Chefin

faul

die Sekretärin

der Angestellte

jemanden entlassen

das Büro(s)	office	**der Angestellte(n)**	employee (m)
die Chefin(nen)	boss (f)	**fleißig**	hard-working
die Sekretärin(nen)	secretary (f)	**faul**	lazy
jemanden einstellen	to employ someone	**aufhören zu arbeiten**	to retire
		jemanden entlassen	to fire someone

der Beruf

der Klempner

der Maurer

der Architekt

der Beruf(e)	job, profession
der Maurer(-)	bricklayer
der Klempner(-)	plumber
der Architekt(en)	architect (m)

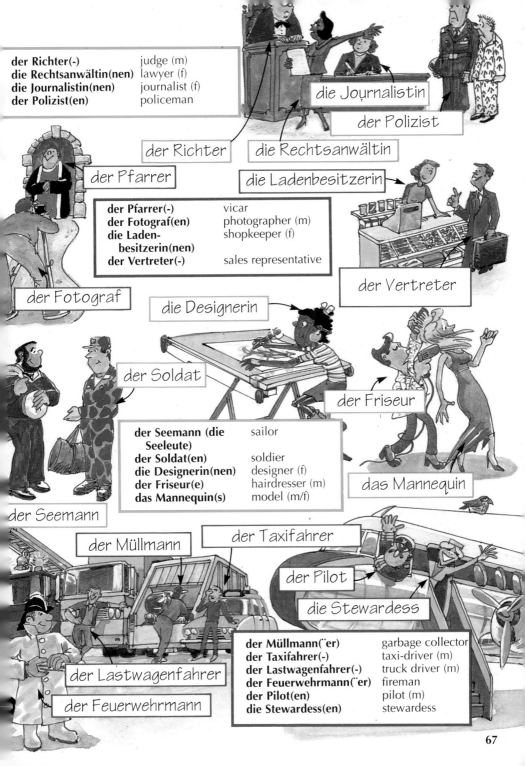

der Richter(-) judge (m)
die Rechtsanwältin(nen) lawyer (f)
die Journalistin(nen) journalist (f)
der Polizist(en) policeman

die Journalistin

der Polizist

der Richter

die Rechtsanwältin

der Pfarrer

die Ladenbesitzerin

der Pfarrer(-) vicar
der Fotograf(en) photographer (m)
**die Laden-
besitzerin(nen)** shopkeeper (f)
der Vertreter(-) sales representative

der Vertreter

der Fotograf

die Designerin

der Soldat

der Friseur

**der Seemann (die
Seeleute)** sailor
der Soldat(en) soldier
die Designerin(nen) designer (f)
der Friseur(e) hairdresser (m)
das Mannequin(s) model (m/f)

das Mannequin

der Seemann

der Müllmann

der Taxifahrer

der Pilot

die Stewardess

der Lastwagenfahrer

der Müllmann(¨er) garbage collector
der Taxifahrer(-) taxi-driver (m)
der Lastwagenfahrer(-) truck driver (m)
der Feuerwehrmann(¨er) fireman
der Pilot(en) pilot (m)
die Stewardess(en) stewardess

der Feuerwehrmann

Illness and health

sich krank fühlen

die Temperatur messen

das Thermometer

Fieber haben

die Ärztin

das Rezept

heilen

sich besser fühlen

die Tablette

gesund

sich krank fühlen	to feel sick	die Ärztin(nen)	doctor (f)
die Temperatur messen	to take someone's temperature	das Rezept(e)	prescription
das Thermometer(-)	thermometer	heilen	to cure
Fieber haben	to have a temperature	die Tablette(n)	pill
		sich besser fühlen	to feel better
		gesund	healthy

eine Erkältung haben

niesen

in Ohnmacht fallen

Bauchweh haben

sich übergeben

Kopfschmerzen haben

eine Erkältung haben	to have a cold
niesen	to sneeze
in Ohnmacht fallen	to faint
Bauchweh haben	to have stomach ache
sich übergeben	to be sick, vomit
Kopfschmerzen haben	to have a headache

der Zahnarzt

sich einen Zahn plombieren lassen

die Spritze

Zahnschmerzen haben

der Zahnarzt(¨e)	dentist (m)
sich einen Zahn plombieren lassen	to have a filling
die Spritze(n)	injection
Zahnschmerzen haben	to have toothache

das Krankenhaus

die Unfallstation

die Verbrennung

sich die Hand verstauchen

der blaue Fleck

sich das Bein brechen

die Schnittwunde

das Heftpflaster

der Verband

das Krankenhaus(¨er)	hospital	**die Verbrennung(en)**	burn
die Unfallstation(en)	emergency room	**sich die Hand verstauchen**	to sprain your wrist
sich das Bein brechen	to break your leg		
der blaue Fleck(en)	bruise	**das Heftpflaster(-)**	adhesive bandage
die Schnittwunde(n)	cut	**der Verband(¨e)**	bandage

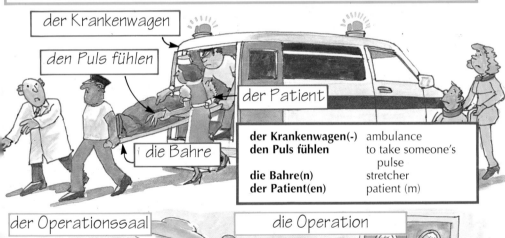

der Krankenwagen

den Puls fühlen

der Patient

die Bahre

der Krankenwagen(-)	ambulance
den Puls fühlen	to take someone's pulse
die Bahre(n)	stretcher
der Patient(en)	patient (m)

der Operationssaal

die Operation

die Krankenschwester

der Chirurg

der Operationssaal	operating theatre
der Chirurg(en)	surgeon (m)
die Operation(en)	operation
die Krankenschwester(n)	nurse (f)

69

School and education

der Kindergarten

die Grundschule

der Direktor

das Gymnasium

die Universität

die Direktorin

der Kindergarten(¨)	nursery school	**das Gymnasium (die Gymnasien)**	high school
die Grundschule(n)	primary school		
der Direktor(en)	director	**die Direktorin(nen)**	headmistress
		die Universität(en)	university

in der Schule

das Klassenzimmer

die Unterrichtsstunde

der Lehrer

die Karte

lehren

der Schüler

lernen

die Tafel

einfach

schwierig

die Kreide

etwas fragen

lesen

schreiben

in der Schule	at school	**lernen**	to learn
das Klassenzimmer(-)	classroom	**einfach**	easy
die Karte(n)	map	**schwierig**	difficult
die Unterrichts-stunde(n)	lesson	**die Tafel(n)**	blackboard
		die Kreide(n)	chalk
der Lehrer(-)	teacher (m)	**lesen**	to read
lehren	to teach	**schreiben**	to write
der Schüler(-)	pupil (m)	**etwas fragen**	to ask a question

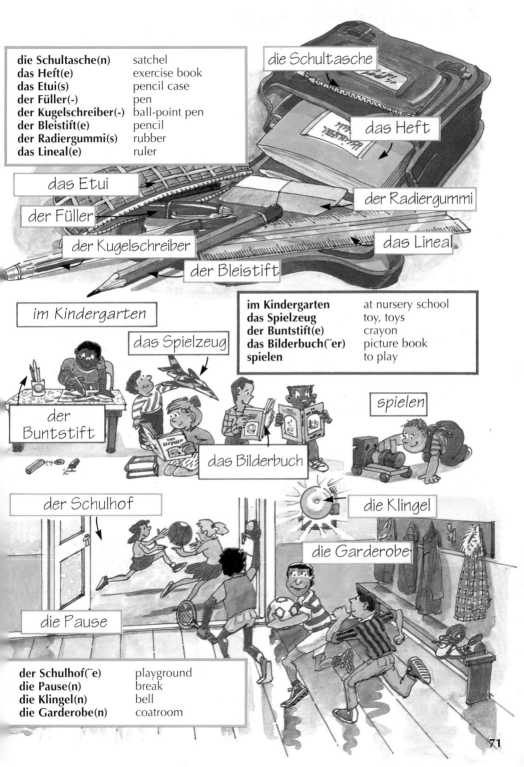

die Schultasche(n)	satchel
das Heft(e)	exercise book
das Etui(s)	pencil case
der Füller(-)	pen
der Kugelschreiber(-)	ball-point pen
der Bleistift(e)	pencil
der Radiergummi(s)	rubber
das Lineal(e)	ruler

die Schultasche

das Heft

das Etui

der Radiergummi

der Füller

das Lineal

der Kugelschreiber

der Bleistift

im Kindergarten

im Kindergarten	at nursery school
das Spielzeug	toy, toys
der Buntstift(e)	crayon
das Bilderbuch(¨er)	picture book
spielen	to play

das Spielzeug

spielen

der Buntstift

das Bilderbuch

der Schulhof

die Klingel

die Garderobe

die Pause

der Schulhof(¨e)	playground
die Pause(n)	break
die Klingel(n)	bell
die Garderobe(n)	coatroom

School and education

das Schulhalbjahr

der Stundenplan

das Fach

der Anfang des Schulhalbjahres

das Ende des Schulhalbjahres

Deutsch

Mathematik

Physik

Englisch

Chemie

Französisch

Biologie

Spanisch

Geschichte

Erdkunde

Musik

Informatik

Sport

das Schulhalbjahr(e)	term	Spanisch	Spanish
der Anfang des Schulhalbjahres	beginning of term	Mathematik	maths
		Physik	physics
das Ende des Schulhalbjahres	end of term	Chemie	chemistry
		Biologie	biology
der Stundenplan(¨e)	timetable	Geschichte	history
das Fach(¨er)	subject	Erdkunde	geography
Deutsch	German	Musik	music
Englisch	English	Informatik	computer studies
Französisch	French	Sport	PE

A B C D E F G H I J K L M N O P Q R S T U V W X Y Z

der Buchstabe

das Alphabet

die Grammatik

die Rechtschreibung

der Großbuchstabe

das Wort

der Satz

der Punkt

der Buchstabe(n)	letter
das Alphabet(e)	alphabet
die Grammatik	grammar
die Rechtschreibung	spelling
der Großbuch-stabe(n)	capital letter
das Wort(¨er)	word
der Satz(¨e)	sentence
der Punkt(e)	full stop

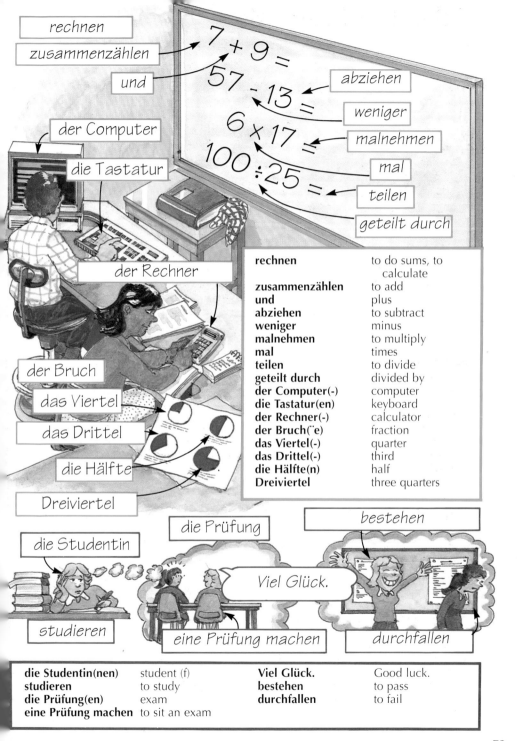

rechnen

zusammenzählen

und

$7 + 9 =$

$57 - 13 =$

abziehen

weniger

$6 \times 17 =$

malnehmen

mal

der Computer

$100 : 25 =$

die Tastatur

teilen

geteilt durch

der Rechner

rechnen	to do sums, to calculate
zusammenzählen	to add
und	plus
abziehen	to subtract
weniger	minus
malnehmen	to multiply
mal	times
teilen	to divide
geteilt durch	divided by
der Computer(-)	computer
die Tastatur(en)	keyboard
der Rechner(-)	calculator
der Bruch(¨e)	fraction
das Viertel(-)	quarter
das Drittel(-)	third
die Hälfte(n)	half
Dreiviertel	three quarters

der Bruch

das Viertel

das Drittel

die Hälfte

Dreiviertel

die Studentin

die Prüfung

bestehen

Viel Glück.

studieren

eine Prüfung machen

durchfallen

die Studentin(nen)	student (f)	Viel Glück.	Good luck.
studieren	to study	bestehen	to pass
die Prüfung(en)	exam	durchfallen	to fail
eine Prüfung machen	to sit an exam		

Shapes and sizes

die Form(en)	shape
der Kreis(e)	circle
das Quadrat(e)	square
das Dreieck(e)	triangle
der Kegel(-)	cone
das Rechteck(e)	rectangle

riesig

groß

klein

winzig

riesig	enormous
groß	big
klein	small
winzig	tiny

die Form

der Kreis

das Quadrat

das Dreieck

der Kegel

das Rechteck

die Größe

messen

der Meter

der Zentimeter

die Länge

die Breite

die Größe(n)	size
messen	to measure
der Meter(-)	meter
der Zentimeter(-)	centimeter
die Länge(n)	length
die Breite(n)	width

der Inhalt

das Gewicht

der Liter

ein halber Liter

das Kilo

ein Pfund

der Inhalt(e)	volume	**das Gewicht(e)**	weight
der Liter(-)	liter	**das Kilo(-)**	kilo
ein halber Liter(-)	half a liter	**ein Pfund(e)**	half a kilo

Numbers

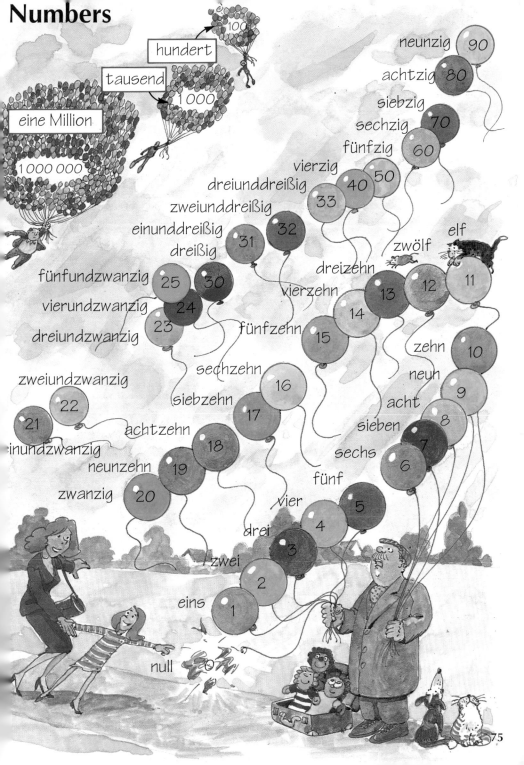

hundert — 100

tausend — 1 000

eine Million — 1 000 000

neunzig — 90
achtzig — 80
siebzig
sechzig — 70
fünfzig — 60
vierzig — 50
dreiunddreißig — 40
zweiunddreißig — 33
einunddreißig — 32
dreißig — 31
fünfundzwanzig — 30
vierundzwanzig — 25
dreiundzwanzig — 24
23
zweiundzwanzig — 22
21
einundzwanzig
neunzehn — 19
achtzehn — 18
siebzehn — 17
sechzehn — 16
fünfzehn — 15
vierzehn — 14
dreizehn — 13
zwölf — 12
elf — 11
zehn — 10
neun — 9
acht — 8
sieben — 7
sechs — 6
fünf — 5
vier — 4
drei — 3
zwei — 2
eins — 1
null — 0
zwanzig — 20

75

Sport

fit halten

trainieren

joggen gehen

das Stirnband

der Trainingsanzug

die Turnschuhe

fit halten	to keep fit	**die Turnschuhe**	gym shoes
trainieren	to exercise	(s: der Turnschuh)	
joggen gehen	to go jogging	**der Trainingsanzug(¨e)**	tracksuit
das Stirnband(¨er)	headband		

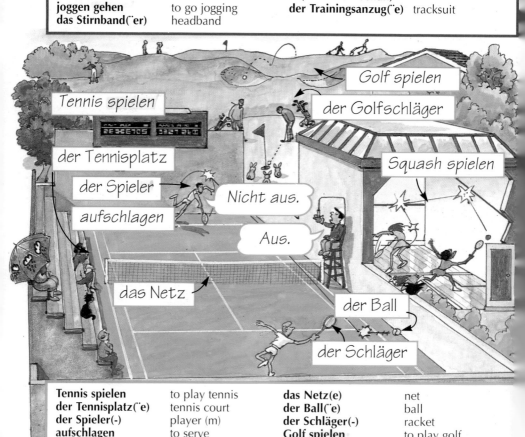

Golf spielen

der Golfschläger

Tennis spielen

der Tennisplatz

Squash spielen

der Spieler

aufschlagen

Nicht aus.

Aus.

das Netz

der Ball

der Schläger

Tennis spielen	to play tennis	**das Netz(e)**	net
der Tennisplatz(¨e)	tennis court	**der Ball(¨e)**	ball
der Spieler(-)	player (m)	**der Schläger(-)**	racket
aufschlagen	to serve	**Golf spielen**	to play golf
Nicht aus.	In.	**der Golfschläger(-)**	golf club
Aus.	Out.	**Squash spielen**	to play squash

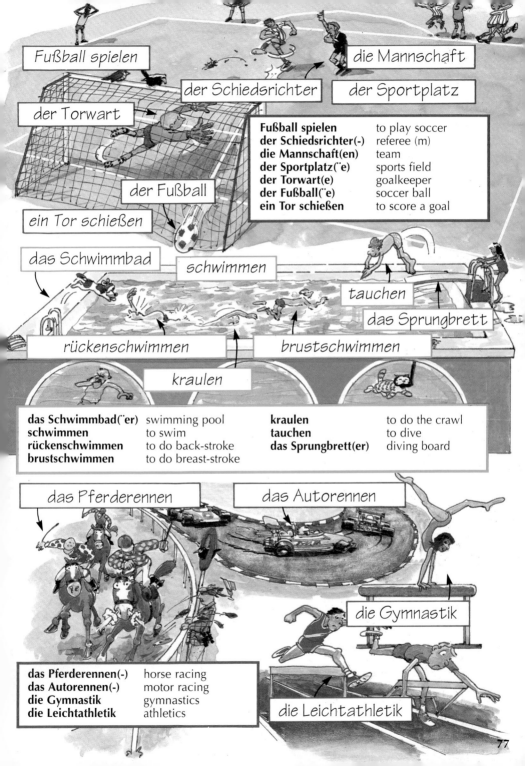

Fußball spielen

die Mannschaft

der Schiedsrichter

der Sportplatz

der Torwart

Fußball spielen	to play soccer
der Schiedsrichter(-)	referee (m)
die Mannschaft(en)	team
der Sportplatz(¨e)	sports field
der Torwart(e)	goalkeeper
der Fußball(¨e)	soccer ball
ein Tor schießen	to score a goal

der Fußball

ein Tor schießen

das Schwimmbad

schwimmen

tauchen

das Sprungbrett

rückenschwimmen

brustschwimmen

kraulen

das Schwimmbad(¨er)	swimming pool	**kraulen**	to do the crawl
schwimmen	to swim	**tauchen**	to dive
rückenschwimmen	to do back-stroke	**das Sprungbrett(er)**	diving board
brustschwimmen	to do breast-stroke		

das Pferderennen

das Autorennen

die Gymnastik

das Pferderennen(-)	horse racing
das Autorennen(-)	motor racing
die Gymnastik	gymnastics
die Leichtathletik	athletics

die Leichtathletik

Celebrations

der Geburtstag(e)	birthday
die Party(s)	party
der Luftballon(s)	balloon
Herzlichen Glückwunsch zum Geburtstag.	Happy Birthday.
einladen	to invite
Spaß haben	to have fun, to enjoy yourself
die Torte(n)	cake
die Kerze(n)	candle
die Karte(n)	card
das Geschenk(e)	present
die Verpackung(en)	wrapping

der Geburtstag

die Party

der Luftballon

Herzlichen Glückwunsch zum Geburtstag.

einladen

Spaß haben

die Torte

die Kerze

das Geschenk

die Verpackung

die Karte

der Heilige Abend

Ostern

Weihnachten

der erste Weihnachstag

der Weihnachtsbaum

Ostern	Easter
Weihnachten	Christmas
der Heilige Abend	Christmas Eve
der erste Weihnachstag	Christmas Day
der Weihnachtsbaum(¨e)	Christmas tree

sich verloben

die Hochzeit

heiraten

der Bräutigam

die Braut

der Gast

gratulieren

der Blumenstrauß

glücklich sein

die Flitterwochen

sich verloben	to get engaged
die Hochzeit(en)	wedding
heiraten	to get married
der Bräutigam(e)	bridegroom
die Braut(¨e)	bride
der Gast(¨e)	guest (m)
gratulieren	to congratulate
der Blumenstrauß(¨e)	bouquet
glücklich sein	to be happy
die Flitterwochen (pl)	honeymoon

Frohe Weihnachten.

das Weihnachtslied

Frohe Weihnachten.	Happy Christmas.
das Weihnachtslied(er)	Christmas carol
schenken	to give (a present)
bekommen	to receive
Danke schön.	Thank you very much.
sich bedanken	to thank

schenken

bekommen

Danke schön.

sich bedanken

Silvester

Neujahr

feiern

Glückliches Neues Jahr.

Silvester	New Year's Eve
Neujahr	New Year's Day
feiern	to celebrate
Glückliches Neues Jahr.	Happy New Year.

Days and dates

der Kalender

der Monat

Januar
Februar
März
April
Mai
Juni
Juli
August
September
Oktober
November
Dezember

das Jahr

Montag
Dienstag
Mittwoch
Donnerstag
Freitag
Samstag
Sonntag

der Tag

die Woche

das Wochenende

der Kalender(-)	calendar
der Monat(e)	month
Januar	January
Februar	February
März	March
April	April
Mai	May
Juni	June
Juli	July
August	August
September	September
Oktober	October
November	November
Dezember	December
das Jahr(e)	year
der Tag(e)	day
die Woche(n)	week
das Wochenende(n)	week-end
Montag(m)	Monday
Dienstag(m)	Tuesday
Mittwoch(m)	Wednesday
Donnerstag(m)	Thursday
Freitag(m)	Friday
Samstag(m)	Saturday
Sonntag(m)	Sunday

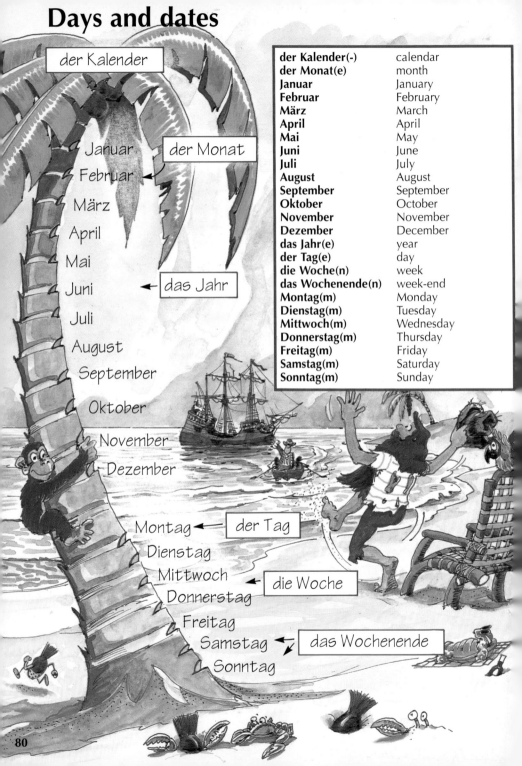

der Kalender(-)	diary
das Datum (pl: Daten)	date
Dienstag, der zweite Juni	Tuesday, the second of June
der erste	the first
der zweite	the second
der dritte	the third
der vierte	the fourth
der fünfte	the fifth

der Kalender

das Datum

Dienstag, der zweite Juni

der erste

der zweite

der dritte

der vierte

der fünfte

1

gestern

gestern Morgen

gestern Abend

4

übermorgen

nächsten Montag

nächste Woche

2

heute

heute Morgen

heute Abend

5

am nächsten Tag

3

morgen

morgen früh

vorgestern

morgen Abend

gestern	yesterday
gestern Morgen	yesterday morning
gestern Abend	yesterday evening
heute	today
heute Morgen	this morning
heute Abend	this evening
morgen	tomorrow
morgen früh	tomorrow morning
morgen Abend	tomorrow evening
vorgestern	the day before yesterday
übermorgen	the day after tomorrow
nächsten Montag	next Monday
nächste Woche	next week
am nächsten Tag	the next day

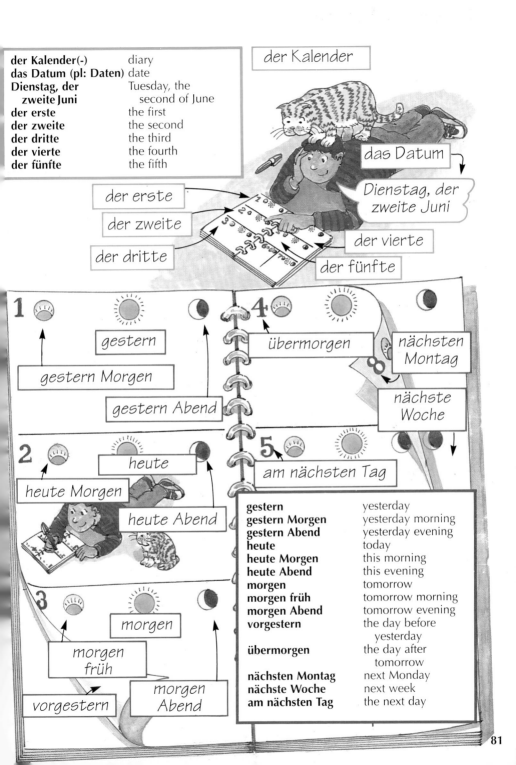

Time

das Morgengrauen(-)	dawn	**die Sonne**	sun
der Sonnenaufgang(¨e)	sunrise	**der Himmel**	sky
Es wird hell.	It is getting light.	**Es ist hell.**	It is light.
der Morgen(-)	morning	**der Tag(e)**	day

der Nachmittag(e)	afternoon	**die Nacht(¨e)**	night
der Abend(e)	evening	**die Sterne (s: der Stern)**	stars
der Sonnenuntergang(¨e)	sunset	**der Mond**	moon
Es wird dunkel.	It is getting dark.	**Es ist dunkel.**	It is dark.

Wie spät ist es?	What time is it?	**Mitternacht**	midnight
die Stunde(n)	hour	**Viertel vor zehn**	a quarter to 10
die Minute(n)	minute	**fünf nach zehn**	five past 10
die Sekunde(n)	second	**Viertel nach zehn**	a quarter past 10
Es ist ein Uhr.	It is 1 o'clock.	**halb elf**	half past 10
Es ist drei Uhr.	It is 3 o'clock.	**acht Uhr morgens**	8 a.m.
Mittag	midday	**acht Uhr abends**	8 p.m.

die Zeit	time	**damals**	in the past
die Vergangenheit	past	**in der Zukunft**	in the future
die Zukunft	future	**jetzt**	now, nowadays
die Gegenwart	present		

Weather and seasons

die Jahreszeit(en)	season
der Frühling	spring
der Sommer	summer
der Herbst	fall
der Winter	winter

die Jahreszeit

der Frühling

das Wetter

Es regnet.

der Winter

der Regen

der Sturm

die Wolke

der Herbst

der Sommer

der Blitz

der Donner

der Regenschirm

der Regenbogen

die Gummistiefel

klatschnass

die Pfütze

der Regentropfen

der Hagel

die Überschwemmung

das Wetter	weather
Es regnet.	It's raining.
der Regen	rain
der Sturm(¨e)	storm
die Wolke(n)	cloud
der Blitz(e)	lightning
der Donner	thunder
der Regenschirm(e)	umbrella
der Regenbogen(-)	rainbow
die Gummistiefel (pl)	rubber boots
klatschnass	soaked to the skin
die Pfütze(n)	puddle
der Regentropfen(-)	raindrop
der Hagel	hail
die Überschwem- mung(en)	flood

das Klima(s) — climate
die Wettervorher- — weather forecast
sage(n)
Wie ist das Wetter? — What is the weather like?

das Klima

die Wettervorhersage

Es ist schön.

Die Sonne scheint.

schwitzen

Wie ist das Wetter?

Mir ist warm.

Es ist schön. — It's fine.
Die Sonne scheint. — The sun is shining.
schwitzen — to sweat
Mir ist warm. — I'm hot.

der Wind

Es ist windig.

der Wind — wind
Es ist windig. — It's windy.
der Nebel — fog
Es ist neblig. — It's foggy.

Es ist kalt.

der Schnee

der Nebel

Es ist neblig.

halb erfroren sein

der Frost

der Schneemann

der Eiszapfen

Es schneit.

Es ist kalt. — It's cold.
halb erfroren sein — to be frozen
der Frost — frost
der Eiszapfen(-) — icicle
der Schnee — snow
der Schneemann(¨er) — snowman
Es schneit. — It's snowing.
tauen — to thaw

tauen

85

World and universe

die Welt

der Nordpol

der Norden

der Atlantik

der Pazifik

der Westen

der Osten

die Wüste

der Äquator

der Dschungel

der Süden

der Südpol

die Welt(en)	world	**der Norden**	north
der Atlantik	Atlantic Ocean	**der Pazifik**	Pacific Ocean
der Westen	west	**der Osten**	east
die Wüste(n)	desert	**der Äquator**	Equator
der Dschungel(-)	jungle	**der Süden**	south
der Nordpol	North Pole	**der Südpol**	South Pole

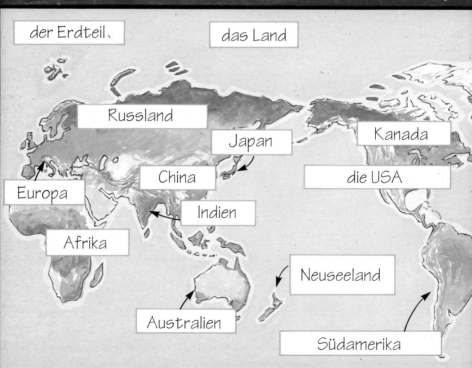

der Erdteil

das Land

Russland

Japan

Kanada

China

die USA

Europa

Indien

Afrika

Neuseeland

Australien

Südamerika

das Universum

der Weltraum

der Stern

der Planet

das Raumschiff

die Milchstraße

das Fernrohr

das Universum	universe
der Weltraum	space
der Planet(en)	planet
der Stern(e)	star
das Raumschiff(e)	spaceship
die Milchstraße(n)	Milky Way
das Fernrohr(e)	telescope

der Erdteil(e)	continent
das Land(¨er)	country
Russland	Russia
Europa	Europe
Afrika	Africa
Japan	Japan
China	China
Indien	India
Australien	Australia
Neuseeland	New Zealand
Kanada	Canada
die USA (pl)	USA
Südamerika	South America

Skandinavien	Scandinavia
Großbritannien	Great Britain
die Niederlande (pl)	Netherlands
Belgien	Belgium
Deutschland	Germany
Frankreich	France
die Schweiz	Switzerland
Italien	Italy
Spanien	Spain

Skandinavien

Großbritannien

die Niederlande

Belgien

Deutschland

Frankreich

die Schweiz

Italien

Spanien

Politics

der Präsident

das Parlament

die Abgeordnete

der Bundeskanzler

die Regierung

der Präsident(en)	president (m)
das Parlament(e)	parliament
die Abgeordnete(n)	member of parliament (f)
der Bundeskanzler(-)*	prime minister (m)
die Regierung(en)	government

die Partei

die Vorsitzende

beliebt

das Mitglied

die Partei(en)	party
die Vorsitzende(n)	leader (f)
beliebt	popular
das Mitglied(er)	member (m/f)

die Wahl

wählen

links

liberal

konservativ

gewinnen

verlieren

Mitglied werden

Mitglied sein

die Wahl(en)	election		liberal	liberal
wählen	to vote		konservativ	right wing
gewinnen	to win		Mitglied werden	to join
verlieren	to loose		Mitglied sein	to belong
links	left wing			

* This is the prime minister (or chancellor) of Germany. For prime ministers of other countries, you say **der Premierminister** or **der Ministerpräsident**.

die Medien (pl)	the media
interviewen	to interview
wichtig	important
interessant	interesting
die Zeitung(en)	newspaper
die Nachrichten (pl)	news
die Schlagzeile(n)	headline
der Artikel(-)	article
wahr	true
falsch	false

die Medien

interviewen

wichtig

interessant

die Zeitung

die Nachrichten

die Schlagzeile

der Artikel

wahr

falsch

#!*&<*
>!!*~!

&#!!

die Politik

der Lohn

die Steuern

die Gesellschaft

die Gewerkschaft

die Arbeitslosigkeit

demokratisch

die Politik	politics	**die Steuern (s: die Steuer)**	taxes
die Gesellschaft	society	**die Gewerkschaft(en)**	trade union
demokratisch	democratic	**die Arbeitslosigkeit**	unemployment
der Lohn(¨e)	wages		

Describing things

laut

ruhig

gehorsam

frech

gleich

unterschiedlich

laut	noisy
ruhig	quiet
gehorsam	obedient
frech	naughty
gleich	same
unterschiedlich	different

beschäftigt

nützlich

zusammen

allein

ängstlich

beschäftigt	busy
nützlich	useful
zusammen	together
allein	alone
ängstlich	frightened
mutig	brave

mutig

unvorsichtig

vorsichtig

böse

lebhaft

zufrieden mit

langweilig

unvorsichtig	careless
vorsichtig	careful
böse	cross
zufrieden mit	pleased with
lebhaft	lively
langweilig	boring

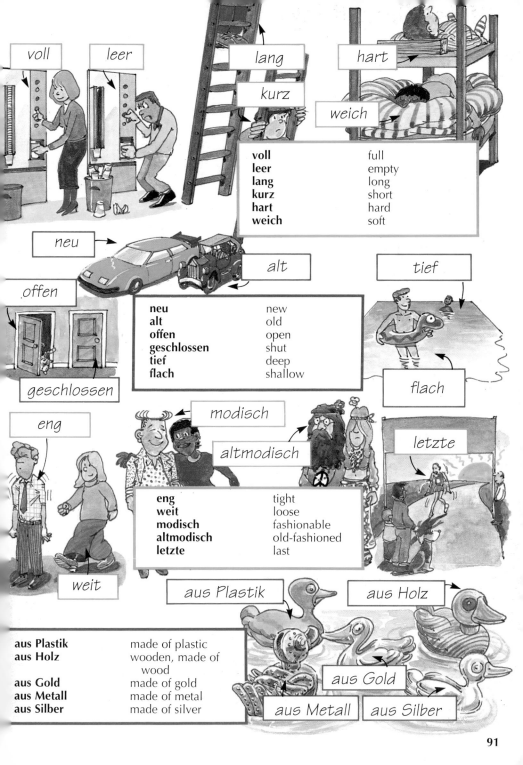

voll

leer

lang

kurz

hart

weich

voll	full
leer	empty
lang	long
kurz	short
hart	hard
weich	soft

neu

alt

tief

offen

neu	new
alt	old
offen	open
geschlossen	shut
tief	deep
flach	shallow

geschlossen

flach

eng

modisch

altmodisch

letzte

eng	tight
weit	loose
modisch	fashionable
altmodisch	old-fashioned
letzte	last

weit

aus Plastik

aus Holz

aus Plastik	made of plastic
aus Holz	wooden, made of wood
aus Gold	made of gold
aus Metall	made of metal
aus Silber	made of silver

aus Gold

aus Metall

aus Silber

Colors

die Farbe

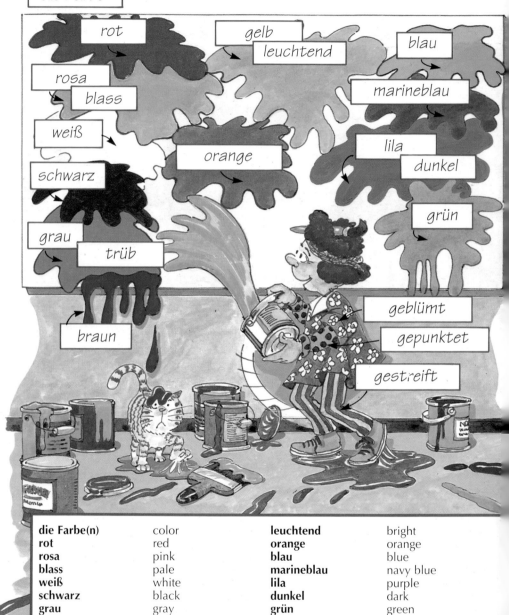

rot
gelb
leuchtend
blau
rosa
blass
marineblau
weiß
orange
lila
dunkel
schwarz
grün
grau
trüb
braun
geblümt
gepunktet
gestreift

die Farbe(n)	color	leuchtend	bright
rot	red	**orange**	orange
rosa	pink	**blau**	blue
blass	pale	**marineblau**	navy blue
weiß	white	**lila**	purple
schwarz	black	**dunkel**	dark
grau	gray	**grün**	green
trüb	dull	**geblümt**	flowered
braun	brown	**gepunktet**	spotted
gelb	yellow	**gestreift**	striped

In, on, under…

in

unter

in

auf

über

aus

neben

nahe an

vor

hinter

zwischen

weit weg von

durch

auf…zu

gegen

zwischen

mit

weg von

hinauf

hinunter

gegenüber

ohne

in (dat)*	in	**gegen (acc)**	against
auf (acc or dat)	on	**durch (acc)**	through
unter (acc or dat)	under	**zwischen (acc or dat)**	among
über (acc or dat)	over	**auf (acc)…zu**	to, towards
in (acc)	into	**weg von (dat)**	away from
aus (dat)	out of	**hinauf (acc. Always follows noun)**	up
neben (acc or dat)	beside		
zwischen (acc or dat)	between	**hinunter (acc. Always follows noun)**	down
nahe an (dat)	near		
weit weg von (dat)	far away from	**gegenüber (dat)**	opposite
vor (acc or dat)	in front of	**mit (dat)**	with
hinter (acc or dat)	behind	**ohne (acc)**	without

*Words like "in" are prepositions. In German they are followed by an accusative or dative noun, as shown in brackets. You can find out more about this on pages 96-98.

Action words

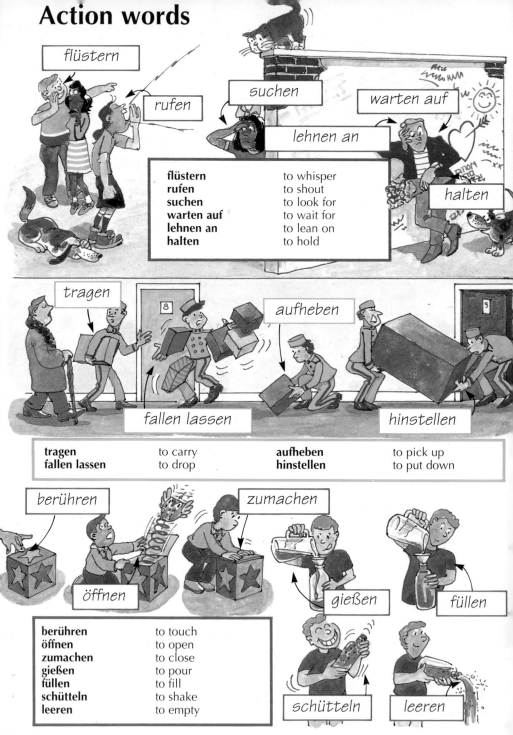

flüstern

rufen

suchen

warten auf

lehnen an

halten

flüstern	to whisper
rufen	to shout
suchen	to look for
warten auf	to wait for
lehnen an	to lean on
halten	to hold

tragen

aufheben

fallen lassen

hinstellen

tragen	to carry	aufheben	to pick up
fallen lassen	to drop	hinstellen	to put down

berühren

zumachen

öffnen

gießen

füllen

schütteln

leeren

berühren	to touch
öffnen	to open
zumachen	to close
gießen	to pour
füllen	to fill
schütteln	to shake
leeren	to empty

zerreißen

werfen

fangen

zerreißen	to tear
flicken	to mend
werfen	to throw
fangen	to catch
umwerfen	to knock over
zerbrechen	to break

flicken

umwerfen

zerbrechen

stehlen

ausrutschen

ziehen

drücken

weglaufen

verfolgen

sich verstecken

ziehen	to pull	**weglaufen**	to run away
drücken	to push	**verfolgen**	to follow
stehlen	to steal	**sich verstecken**	to hide
ausrutschen	to slip		

Grammar hints

In order to speak German well, you need to learn a bit about the grammar, that is, how words fit together and work in sentences. On the next few pages, there are some hints on German grammar. Some of its rules are quite complicated, so don't worry if you cannot remember them all at first. Try to learn a little grammar at a time and then practice using it.

Nouns

In German, all nouns begin with a capital letter and are either masculine, feminine or neuter (this is called their gender). The word you use for "the" shows which gender they are. It is **der** before masculine nouns, **die** before feminine nouns and **das** before neuter nouns:

der Mann	the man (m)
die Frau	the woman (f)
das Kind	the child (n)

Some nouns have a masculine and a feminine form. These are often nouns which describe what people are or what they do:

der Arzt	the doctor (m)
die Ärztin	the doctor (f)
der Journalist	the journalist (m)
die Journalistin	the journalist (f)

When they appear in the illustrated section of this book, only the form which matches the picture is given, but both masculine and feminine forms are given in the word list at the back.

Plurals

When you are talking about more than one thing, the word for "the" is **die**. German nouns often change their endings in the plural and sometimes add an umlaut (¨):

der Mann becomes **die Männer**
die Frau becomes **die Frauen**
das Kind becomes **die Kinder**

It is a good idea when you are learning nouns to learn the plural as well. In this book the plurals are given in brackets after the nouns, e.g. **der Mann(¨er)**.

Cases

In German, nouns have four forms, or cases, depending on what job they do in the sentence. The cases are:

Nominative – a noun is nominative when it is the subject of the sentence (when it is the person or thing doing the action).

Accusative – a noun is accusative when it is the direct object of the sentence (when it is the person or thing to whom the action is done).

Genitive – a noun is genitive when it tells you to whom something belongs (in English, it often has an "'s" after it, e.g. The cat's whiskers).

Dative – a noun is dative when it is the indirect object of the sentence (when it is the person or thing to whom or for whom the action is being done).

Nominative: **The dog** bites the boy.
Accusative: The boy hits **the dog**.
Genitive: **The dog's** eyes look sad.
Dative: The boy gives **the dog** a bone.

der, die, das

The word for "the" changes depending on the case of the noun and on whether the noun is masculine, feminine, neuter or plural. It is a good idea to learn all the cases of **der**, **die** and **das** in lists as shown below:

	singular			plural
---	m	f	n	
Nom	der	die	das	die
Acc	den	die	das	die
Gen	des	der	des	der
Dat	dem	der	dem	den

Occasionally, the noun also changes when it is in a particular case. For example, in the masculine and neuter genitive singular:

der Mann becomes **des Mannes**
das Kind becomes **des Kindes**

ein, eine, ein

The word for "a" or "an" is **ein** before masculine and neuter nouns and **eine** before feminine nouns. **Ein**, **eine** and **ein**, like **der**, **die** and **das**, change depending on the case of the noun. It is best to learn the changes by heart:

	m	f	n
Nom	ein	eine	ein
Acc	einen	eine	ein
Gen	eines	einer	eines
Dat	einem	einer	einem

kein, keine, kein

The word **kein** means "no" or "not a":

Ich habe kein Geld.
I have no money.

In the singular, **kein** changes like **ein**, **eine**, **ein**. The plural is also shown here:

	singular			plural
---	m	f	n	
Nom	kein	keine	kein	keine
Acc	keinen	keine	kein	keine
Gen	keines	keiner	keines	keiner
Dat	keinem	keiner	keinem	keinen

dieser, diese, dieses

To say "this" in German, you use **dieser**:

dieser Mann   this man

Dieser changes like **der**, **die**, **das**:

	singular			plural
---	m	f	n	
Nom	dieser	diese	dieses	diese
Acc	diesen	diese	dieses	diese
Gen	dieses	dieser	dieses	dieser
Dat	diesem	dieser	diesem	diesen

mein, dein, sein

Mein (my), **dein** (your), **sein** (his, her, its) and so on are called possessive adjectives. They have the same endings as **ein** and **kein** (see over).

m	f	n	
mein	meine	mein	my
dein	deine	dein	your (s)
sein	seine	sein	his, its
ihr	ihre	ihr	her
unser	unsere	unser	our
euer	eure	euer	your (pl)
ihr	ihre	ihr	their
Ihr	Ihre	Ihr	your (s and pl polite)*

Here are some examples of how to use "my", "your", etc in German:

Ich liebe meinen Hund.
I love my dog.
Sie spielt mit ihrer Katze.
She is playing with her cat.
Wir besuchen unsere Großeltern.
We are visiting our grandparents.
Er fährt auf meinem Rad.
He is riding my bicycle.

Prepositions

Prepositions are words which tell you where things are (e.g. under the table), where things are going (e.g. the train to Hamburg; the card is for you) or when they will happen (e.g. on Friday). In German, prepositions are followed either by an accusative or a dative:

durch (acc) through:
Die Katze springt durch das Fenster.
The cat leaps through the window.

aus (dat) out of:
Die Katze springt aus dem Korb. The cat leaps out of the basket.

A few prepositions can take either case. They take the accusative when a change of place or a movement is involved (e.g. The cat ran under the table), and the dative when there is no change of place or no movement (e.g. The cat is sleeping under the table):

auf (acc) on:
Mein Hut ist auf den Tisch gefallen.
My hat fell onto the table.

auf (dat) on:
Mein Hut liegt auf dem Tisch.
My hat is on the table.

There is a list of prepositions on page 93 which tells you which case each takes. The cases are also shown in the word list at the back.

Adjectives

Adjectives are words which describe a noun. They too have different endings depending on which case the noun is in and whether they are used with **der, die, das** or **ein, eine, ein.**

With **der, die, das:**

singular	m	f
Nom	**der junge**	die junge
Acc	**den jungen**	die junge
Gen	**des jungen**	der jungen
Dat	**dem jungen**	der jungen

	n	plural
Nom	**das junge**	die jungen
Acc	**das jungen**	die jungen
Gen	**des jungen**	der jungen
Dat	**dem jungen**	den jungen

der junge Mann the young man
die grünen Äpfel the green apples

With ein, eine, ein:

singular m		f
Nom	**ein junger**	**eine junge**
Acc	**einen jungen**	**eine junge**
Gen	**eines jungen**	**einer jungen**
Dat	**einem jungen**	**einer jungen**

	n	plural
Nom	**ein junges**	**junge**
Acc	**ein junges**	**junge**
Gen	**eines jungen**	**junger**
Dat	**einem jungen**	**jungen**

ein roter Lutballon a red balloon
ein hübsches Mädchen a pretty girl

Adjectives with **kein, mein, dein**, etc have the same endings as they do with **ein** in the singular. In the plural, they end with "en" whatever the case:

mein neues Fahrrad my new bicycle
deine kleine Schwester your little sister
keine roten Schuhe no red shoes

Comparing adjectives

When you compare things in German, the adjectives change in the same way as English ones, adding "er" or "est/st":

frisch	fresh
frischer	fresher
frischest	freshest

Often you also add an umlaut (¨) when the adjective is short and has just one syllable:

jung	young
jünger	younger
jüngst	youngest

These adjectives take the same endings as ordinary ones:

der frischeste Apfel the freshest apple

Some common adjectives change completely as they do in English:

gut	good	**viel**	many
besser	better	**mehr**	more
best	best	**meist**	most

Pronouns

"I", "you", "he", "she" and so on are called subject pronouns. You use them in place of a nominative noun (one which is the subject of a sentence). Here are the nominative pronouns:

ich	I	**wir**	we
du	you (s)	**ihr**	you (pl)
er	he	**sie**	they
sie	she	**Sie**	you (s and pl
es	it		polite)

In German, there are three words for you: **du, ihr** and **Sie**. For people you know well, such as friends and family, you use **du** in the singular and **ihr** in the plural. **Sie** is a polite form that you use with people you do not know very well. When it means you, **Sie** is always spelt with a capital "S".

An object pronoun is one which you put in place of a noun which is the object of the sentence. German pronouns have cases just like nouns: there are accusative ones to replace a direct object, and dative ones to replace an indirect object.

Here are the accusative pronouns:

mich	me
dich	you (s)
ihn	him
sie	her
es	it
uns	us
euch	you (pl)
sie	they
Sie	you (s and pl polite)

The following is a list of the dative pronouns:

mir	to/for me
dir	to/for you (s)
ihm	to/for him
ihr	to/for her
ihm	to/for it
uns	to/for us
euch	to/for your (pl)
ihnen	to/for them
Ihnen	to/for you (s and pl polite)

Verbs

Verbs are 'doing' or action words. They change their endings depending on who is doing the action. In German most verbs follow a regular pattern. You take the "en" off the infinitive then add the different endings. These are the endings for the present tense:

infinitive: **hören** to hear

ich hör -e	I hear/am hearing
du hör -st	
er/sie/es hör -t	
wir hör -en	
ihr hör -t	
sie hör -en	
Sie hör -en	

Verbs like **hören** are called weak verbs. There are other verbs, like **geben**, which change the vowel in the **du** and **er** forms of the present tense. These belong to a group of verbs called strong verbs:

geben   to give

ich geb -e
du gib -st
er/sie/es gib -t
wir geb -en
ihr geb -t
sie geb -en
Sie geb -en

You can find a list of strong verbs on page 105.

Some very common verbs, such as **sein** (to be) and **haben** (to have) do not take the normal pattern of endings. They are known as irregular verbs and it is best to learn them as you come across them. The present tenses of **sein** and **haben** are shown below. You can find the present tenses of other irregular verbs on pages 103-104.

sein to be	**haben** to have
ich bin	**ich habe**
du bist	**du hast**
er/sie/es ist	**er/sie/es hat**
wir sind	**wir haben**
ihr seid	**ihr habt**
sie sind	**sie haben**
Sie sind	**Sie haben**

The future tense is used for things you are going to do. In German you make the future by putting the infinitive with the present tense of the verb **werden**.

Werden means "to become". When it is used to make the future, **werden** is equivalent to "shall" or "will" in English. **Werden** is a strong verb:

ich werde essen   I will eat
du wirst essen
er/sie/es wird essen
wir werden essen
ihr werdet essen
sie werden essen
Sie werden essen

You use the perfect tense for events which have already happened ("I have danced", "I danced", in English). In German the perfect is made by putting **haben** with the past participle of the verb. The past participle is based on the infinitive. For weak verbs you take the "en" off the infinitive, add "ge" at the beginning and "t" or "et" at the end:

	infinitive	past participle
to hear	**hören**	**gehört**
to play	**spielen**	**gespielt**
to wait	**warten**	**gewartet**

Strong verbs keep the "en" ending of the infinitive, add "ge" at the beginning and often change the vowel:

	infinitive	past participle
to give	**geben**	**gegeben**
to find	**finden**	**gefunden**
to see	**sehen**	**gesehen**

The list of strong verbs on page 105 shows their past participles. It is best to try and learn them by heart.

Here is the perfect tense of hören:

ich habe gehört
du hast gehört
er/sie/es hat gehört
wir haben gehört
ihr habt gehört
sie haben gehört
Sie haben gehört

A few German verbs use **sein** rather than **haben** to make the perfect tense:
ich bin gekommen I came
ich bin gefahren I went, I traveled

They are usually verbs which involve movement or change of some kind. There is a list of common verbs which take **sein** on page 104.

Separable verbs

Some German verbs are made up of two parts which are separated in a sentence. For example, **ankommen** (to arrive) is made up of **an** (in, at) and **kommen** (to come). **Kommen** is used like a normal verb, but you usually put **an** (called the prefix) at the end of the sentence:

Der Zug kommt um vier Uhr an.
The train arrives at four o'clock.

In the perfect tense, the "ge" of the past participle comes between the prefix and the main part of the verb:

Der Zug ist um vier Uhr angekommen. The train arrived at four o'clock.

Here is a list of the prefixes of separable verbs. If a verb begins with any of these you know that it separates:

ab	off	**los**	away
an	at, on	**mit**	with
auf	up	**nach**	after
aus	out	**vor**	before
ein	in, into	**weg**	away
her	here	**zu**	to
hin	there, away	**zurück**	back

Reflexive verbs

Reflexive verbs are made up of a verb and the pronoun **sich**. **Sich** means "self" and reflexive verbs often involve doing something to yourself:

sich waschen to wash oneself
sich setzen to sit down

The pronoun **sich** changes depending on who is doing the action:

ich wasche mich
du wäscht dich
er/sie/es wäscht sich
wir waschen uns
ihr wascht euch
sie waschen sich
Sie waschen sich

You use **haben** to make the perfect tense of reflexive verbs.

ich habe mich gewaschen

Word order

In a German sentence, the words are in a different order from those in an English sentence. The verb is always the second idea in the sentence with the subject usually first and the object third. Other words or ideas follow in order of time, manner, then place:

Sie liest ein Buch.
She is reading a book.
Sie liest mir das Buch vor.
She is reading the book to me.
Wir fliegen nach Berlin.
We are flying to Berlin.
Wir fahren nächste Woche mit dem Auto nach Berlin. We are going to Berlin by car next week.

In the future and perfect tenses, the infinitive and past participle go right to the end of the sentence:

Ich werde eine Party geben.
I am going to have a party.
Er hat seine Brieftasche gefunden.
He has found his wallet.

Negatives

To make a negative in German, you put **nicht** ("not") after the verb:

Er spricht nicht laut.
He is not speaking loudly.
Ich werde nicht ausgehen.
I will not go out.

In the perfect tense the **nicht** comes just before the past participle:

Ich habe das Eis nicht gegessen.
I did not eat the ice-cream.

The word **kein** ("no" or "not a", see page 97) is used with nouns to make negatives:

Ich habe keine Katze. I do not have a cat./I have no cat.

Questions

To form a question, you put the subject after the verb, as in English:

Hast du ein neues Kleid?
Have you/Do you have a new dress?
Wird deine Schwester auch kommen?
Will your sister come too?

Here are some questions beginning with common question words:

Wer ist das? Who is that?
Was machst du? What are you doing?
Wann ist sie nach Frankfurt gefahren?
When did she go to Frankfurt?
Wie bist du hierher gekommen?
How did you get here?
Wie viel kostet die Fahrkarte?
How much does the ticket cost?
Wie viele Brüder hast du?
How many brothers have you got?
Warum hat sie das gesagt?
Why did she say that?
Wo ist das Kino?
Where is the cinema?
Woher kommst du?
Where do you come from?

Welcher means "which" or "what". It changes like **dieser, diese, dieses** to agree with the noun which follows:

Welches Buch liest du?
What book are you reading?

Welche Sprachen kennt er?
Which languages does he know?

Irregular verbs

Here are the present tenses of some very useful common irregular verbs.

dürfen to be allowed to

ich darf
du darfst
er/sie/es darf
wir dürfen
ihr dürft
sie dürfen
Sie dürfen

können to be able to

ich kann
du kannst
er/sie/es kann
wir können
ihr könnt
sie können
Sie können

mögen to like

ich mag
du magst
er/sie/es mag
wir mögen
ihr mögt
sie mögen
Sie mögen

müssen to have to

ich muss
du musst
er/sie/es muss
ihr müßt
sie müssen
Sie müssen

sollen to be expected to, to have to

ich soll
du sollst
er/sie/es soll
wir sollen
ihr sollt
sie sollen
Sie sollen

wissen to know

ich weiß
du weißt
er/sie/es weiß
wir wissen
ihr wisst
sie wissen
Sie wissen

wollen to want to, to intend to

ich will
du willst
er/sie/es will
wir wollen
ihr wollt
sie wollen
Sie wollen

These are verbs which make their perfect with **sein**:

ankommen	to arrive
aufstehen	to get up
aufwachen	to wake up
begegnen	to meet
bleiben	to stay
einschlafen	to fall asleep
erscheinen	to appear
erschrecken	to be frightened
fahren	to go (by a means of transport), to drive
fallen	to fall
fliegen	to fly
folgen	to follow
gehen	to go (on foot)
gelingen	to succeed
geschehen	to happen
klettern	to climb
kommen	to come
misslingen	to fail
passieren	to happen
schmelzen	to melt
schwimmen	to swim
segeln	to sail
Ski laufen	to ski
steigen	to climb, to go up
sterben	to die
vergehen	to pass, to go by
wachsen	to grow
werden	to become

Strong verbs

Here is a list of common strong verbs. The parts given are the infinitive and the **er** form of the present and the perfect tenses. Try to learn these three parts for every strong verb.

beginnen	beginnt	hat begonnen	to begin
bitten	bittet	hat gebeten	to ask
bleiben	bleibt	ist geblieben	to stay
essen	isst	hat gegessen	to eat
fahren	fährt	ist gefahren	to go, to drive
finden	findet	hat gefunden	to find
geben	gibt	hat gegeben	to give
gehen	geht	ist gegangen	to go
geschehen	geschieht	ist geschehen	to happen
halten	hält	hat gehalten	to hold
heißen	heißt	hat geheißen	to be called
helfen	hilft	hat geholfen	to help
kommen	kommt	ist gekommen	to come
lassen	läßt	hat gelassen	to leave
laufen	läuft	ist gelaufen	to run
lesen	liest	hat gelesen	to read
liegen	liegt	hat gelegen	to lie
nehmen	nimmt	hat genommen	to take
rufen	ruft	hat gerufen	to call
scheinen	scheint	hat geschienen	to seem
schlafen	schläft	hat geschlafen	to sleep
schließen	schließt	hat geschlossen	to shut
schreiben	schreibt	hat geschrieben	to write
schwimmen	schwimmt	ist geschwommen	to swim
sehen	sieht	hat gesehen	to see
sein	ist	ist gewesen	to be
singen	singt	hat gesungen	to sing
sitzen	sitzt	hat gesessen	to sit
sprechen	spricht	hat gesprochen	to speak
stehen	steht	hat gestanden	to stand
steigen	steigt	ist gestiegen	to climb, to rise
sterben	stirbt	ist gestorben	to die
tragen	trägt	hat getragen	to carry, to wear
treffen	trifft	hat getroffen	to meet
trinken	trinkt	hat getrunken	to drink
tun	tut	hat getan	to do
verlieren	verliert	hat verloren	to lose
waschen	wäscht	hat gewaschen	to wash
werden	wird	ist geworden	to become
werfen	wirft	hat geworfen	to throw

Phrase explainer

Throughout the illustrated section of this book, there are useful short phrases and everyday expressions. You may find these easier to remember if you understand the different words that make them up.

This section lists the expressions under the page number where they appeared (although those whose word for word meaning is like the English have been left out). After reminding you of the suggested English equivalent, it shows you how they break down and, wherever possible, gives you the literal translations of the words involved*. Any grammatical terms used (e.g. accusative) are explained in the grammar section.

page 4
• **Auf Wiedersehen** Goodbye:
auf=on; **wieder**=again; **sehen**=to see
• **Bis bald**. See you later:
bis=until, **bald**=soon
• **Wie geht's?** How are you?
Wie=how; **geht**=goes; **es**=it (**es** is abbreviated to **'s**).

page 5
• **Das meine ich auch.** I agree:
das=that; **ich meine**=I think; **auch**=also
• **Wie heißt du?** What's your name?
• **Ich heiße...** My name is...
• **Er heißt...** His name is...
wie=how; **heißen**=to be called; **du heißt**=you are called; **ich heiße**=I am called; **er heißt**=he is called.

page 12
• **Ich bin zu Hause.** I'm at home:
ich bin=I am; **zu Hause**=at home (**das Haus**= house).

page 18
• **Vorsicht bissiger Hund!** Beware of the dog!
die Vorsicht=care, caution; **bissig**=biting, vicious; **der Hund**=dog.

page 20
• **Guten Morgen** Good morning: for greetings, you use **gut** with the time of day.

page 25
• **Gute Nacht** Good-night: See above.

page 26
• **Das Essen ist fertig**. It's ready:
das Essen=the meal; **ist fertig**=is ready.
• **Greif zu**. Help yourself:
zugreifen=to dig in, to grab.
• **Guten Appetit.** Enjoy your meal:
gut=good; **der Appetit**=appetite. This is a polite phrase you say to people who are about to eat.

page 36
• **Zugabe!** Encore!
die Zugabe=extra, bonus, addition.

page 37
• **Was hätten Sie gerne?** What would you like?
was=what; **Sie hätten**=you would have (**Sie** is the polite form of "you" singular); **gerne** (or **gern**)=with pleasure, willingly.
• **Mit Bedienung?** Service included?
mit=with; **die Bedienung**=service
• **Ohne Bedienung!** Service not included!
ohne=without.

page 43
• **Wie viel macht das?** How much is that?
wie viel=how much; **machen**=to

106 *Literal meanings of German words are introduced by the sign =.

make; **das**=that; (**kosten**=to cost, can be used instead of **machen: wie viel kostet das?**)
- **Das macht...** That will be...
das macht=that makes, e.g. **Das macht fünf Mark**=That will be five marks; (you could also say **Das kostet...** See below, under page 44).
- **Ein Kilo...** A kilo of...
- **Ein Pfund...** Half a kilo of...
e.g. **Ein Kilo Äpfel, bitte**=A kilo of apples, please. Note that the German word for "pound" means half a kilo.

page 44
- **Das ist preiswert.** It's good value: **das ist**=that is; **preiswert**=good value.
- **Womit kann ich dienen?** Can I help you? **womit**=with what; **kann ich**=can I; **dienen**=serve.
- **Ich hätte gern...** I'd like... (See note above for **Was hätten Sie gerne?** page 37); **ich hätte**=I would have; **gern(e)**=with pleasure, willingly.
- **Welche Größe ist es?** Which size is this? **welche**=which; **die Größe**=size; **es ist**=it is
- **Was kostet...?** How much is...?
- **Das kostet...** It costs...
was=what; **kosten**=to cost, e.g. **Was kostet das T-Shirt?** How much is the T-Shirt?

page 47
- **Haben Sie Kleingeld?** Have you any small change?
haben=to have (**Sie**=polite form of "you" singular); **das Kleingeld** derives from **klein**=small and **das Geld**=money.

page 48
- **Hier ist Anke.** It's Anke: **hier**=here; **ist**=is.

- **Ich rufe dich zurück.** I'll call you back:
rufen=to call; **ich rufe**=I call (note that the present tense is used); **dich**=you (accusative).
- **Wiederhören** Goodbye: **wieder**=again, **hören**=to hear (only used on the telephone).

page 49
- **Sehr geehrte Damen und Herren,** Dear Sir/Madam,
sehr=very; **geehrt**=honoured; **Dame**=lady, Madam; **und**=and; **Herr**=gentleman, sir. This is how you begin a formal letter.
- **Beigefügt finden Sie** I enclose: **beigefügt**=enclosed, added; **find**=to find; **Sie**=polite singular "you".
- **Mit freundlichen Grüßen** Yours faithfully: **mit**=with; **freundlich** =friendly; **der Gruß(¨e)**=greeting.
- **Schön, mal wieder von dir zu hören.** It was lovely to hear from you: **schön**=lovely, good; **mal wieder**=once again; **von dir**=from you; **zu**=to; **hören**=to hear.
- **Mit getrennter Post erhältst du...** I am sending... separately: **mit**=with; **getrennt**=separate; **erhalten**=to receive; **du erhältst**=you receive.
- **Alles Gute...** Love from... =all that is good; all the best.
- **Es ist ganz toll hier.** Having a lovely time:
es ist=it is; **ganz**=very, really; **toll**=great, good; **hier**=here.

- **Schade, dass du nicht hier bist.** Wish you were here:
schade=a shame, a pity; **dass**=that; **du bist**=you are; **nicht**=not.
- **Dringend stop sofort zu Hause anrufen stop** Urgent message stop

phone home stop:
dringend=urgent; **sofort**=immediately; **zu Hause**=home, at home; **anrufen**=to ring/telephone.

page 50
• **In welcher Richtung ist...?** Which way is...?
in=in; **welcher**=which; **die Richtung**=direction; **ist**=is.

page 52
• **Parkverbot!** No parking!
parken=to park; **das Verbot**=ban.

page 54
• **Nichtraucher** No smoking:
nicht=not/non; **der Raucher**=smoker.

page 57
• **Bitte anschnallen.** Please fasten your seatbelts:
bitte=please; **anschnallen**= to strap on/up, to clip on. Note how the infinitive is used to give a polite order.

page 58
• **etwas besichtigen** to sightsee:
etwas=something (also=some, any, a little); **besichtigen**=to look at.

page 73
Viel Glück. Good luck:
viel=much; **das Glück**=luck, happiness.

page 78
• **Herzlichen Glückwunsch zum Geburtstag.** Happy birthday:
herzlich=warm, sincere; **der Glückwunsch(¨e)**=congratualtions (from **das Glück**=luck and **der Wunsch**=wish); **zum** (short for **zu dem**) **Geburtstag**=for the birthday.

• **Danke schön.** Thank you very much:
danke=thanks; **schöne**=nice, beautiful, good (here it simply means "very much", similar to "thank you").
• **Glückliches Neues Jahr.** Happy New Year:
glücklich=happy; **neu**=new; **das Jahr**=year.

page 82
• **Es wird hell/dunkel.** It's getting light/dark.
• **Es ist hell/dunkel.** It is light/dark:
es wird=it is becoming (from **werden**=to become); **es ist**=it is; **hell**=light; **dunkel**=dark.

page 83
• **Wie spät ist es?** What is the time?
wie=how; **spät**=late; **ist es**=is it.
• **Es ist ein/drei Uhr.** It is 1/3 o'clock:
die Uhr=clock, watch.
• **Viertel vor zehn** a quarter to 10:
Viertel=quarter; **vor**=before; **zehn**=ten.
• **Viertel/fünf nach zehn** a quarter/ five past 10:
nach=past, after.
• **halb elf** half past 10:
halb=half; **elf**=eleven (Note that this does not mean "half past eleven").
• **acht Uhr morgens/abends** 8 am/pm:
acht Uhr=eight o'clock; **morgens**=in the morning; **abends**=in the evening.

page 85
• **Wie ist das Wetter?** What is the weather like?
=how is the weather?
• **Mir ist warm.** I'm hot:
mir ist=it is to me, I feel; **warm**=warm.

English-German word list

Here you will find all the German words, phrases and expressions from the illustrated section of this book, listed in English alphabetical order. Wherever useful, phrases and expressions are cross-referenced, and the words they are made up from are included in the list. Following each German term, you will find its pronunciation in italics. To pronounce German properly, you need to listen to a German person speaking. This pronunciation guide will give you an idea as to how to pronounce new words and act as reminder to words you have heard spoken. Remember that the German **ß** is like ss, **w** is like an English v, **v** is like an English f, **z** is like ts and **j** is like y in "yawn".

When using the pronunciation hints in italics, read the "words" as if they were English but bear in mind the following points:
- *ah* should be said like the a in "farther"
- *a* like *ah*, but shorter
- *ow* like ow in "now" (not in "crow")
- *ew* is not quike like any English sound. It is like a sharp u. To make it, say "ee", but keep your lips rounded
- *ee* should be said like ee in "week"
- *ay* should be said like in "day", and *oy* like in "boy"; otherwise *y* is like in "try", except before a vowel when it should be said like in "yawn"
- *g* is always hard, as in "garden"
- *kh* should be said like ch in the Scottish word "loch" or h in "huge"
- *r* is made at the back of the mouth and sounds a litte like gargling
- *e(r)* is like e in "the" (not "thee"), and the *r* is not pronounced
- *u(r)* is like the i in "bird", and the *r* is not pronounced.

A

accident	der Unfall("er)	derr oonfal
actor	der Schauspieler(-)	derr shaow-shpeeler
actress	die Schauspielerin(nen)	dee shaow-shpeelerin
to add	zusammenzählen	tsoo-zammen-tsehlen
address	die Adresse(n)	dee addresse(r)
adhesive bandage	das Heftpflaster(-)	das heft-pflaster
advertisement	die Reklame(n)	dee reklame(r)
Africa	Afrika	Africa
afternoon	der Nachmittag(e)	der nakh-mittakh
against	gegen (acc)	gay-gen
age	das Alter(-)	dass al-ter
I agree, agreed	Das meine ich auch.	dass meyne(r) ikh owkh
airline ticket	der Flugschein(e)	derr floog-shyne
airmail	Luftpost	looftpost
airplane	das Flugzeug(e)	dass floog-tsyok
airport	der Flughafen(")	derr floog-hahfen
aisle	der Gang("e)	derr gang
alarm clock	der Wecker(-)	derr vecker
alone	allein	a-lyne
alphabet	das Alphabet(e)	dass alphabayt
ambulance	der Krankenwagen(-)	derr kranken-vahgen
among	zwischen (acc or dat)	tsvishen
anchor	der Anker(-)	derr anker
and	und	oont
animal	das Tier(e)	dass teer
ankle	der Knöchel(-)	der knu(r)kh-el
to answer the telephone	ans Telefon gehen	anss telephone gayen
apartment	die Wohnung(en)	dee vonoong
block of apartments	der Wohnblock("e)	derr vone-block
apple	der Apfel(")	derr apfel
apple tree	der Apfelbaum("e)	derr apfel-bowm
apricot	die Aprikose(n)	dee aprreekose(r)
April	April	a-prill
architect (m)	der Architekt(en)	derr arkhee-tekt
architect (f)	die Architektin(nen)	dee arkhee-tetkin
area code	die Vorwahl(en)	dee vor-vahl
arm	der Arm(e)	derr arm
armchair	der Sessel(-)	derr zessel
Arrivals	Ankunft (f)	an-koonft
art gallery	die Kunstgalerie(n)	dee koonst-gallerie
article (in paper)	der Artikel(-)	derr arteekel
to ask	fragen	fra-gen
to ask a question	etwas fragen	etvass fragen
to ask the way	nach dem Weg fragen	nakh dym veg fra-gen
to fall asleep	einschlafen	yne-shlaf-en
at the seaside	am Meer	am mayr
athletics	die Leichtathletik	dee lykht-etlytik
Atlantic Ocean	der Atlantik	derr atlantic
attic	der Dachboden(")	derr dakh-boden
audience	das Publikum	dass pooblikoom
August	August	ow-goost
aunt	die Tante(n)	dee tante(r)
Australia	Australien	owstra-lian
away from	weg von (dat)	veck fon

B

baby	das Baby(s)	dass baby
back	der Rücken	derr rewken
to do back-stroke	rückenschwimmen	rewken-shvimmen
backward	rückwärts	rewk-verts
bag	die Tragetasche(n)	dee trahge-tashe
bait	der Köder(-)	derr koyder
baker	der Bäcker	derr becker
balcony	der Balkon(s)	derrr bal-cone
with balcony	mit Balkon	mit bal-cone
bald head	die Glatze(n)	dee glatse(r)
to be bald	eine Glatze haben	yne glatse haben
ball	der Ball(¨e)	derr bal
ballet	das Ballet	dass bailett
ballet dancer (m)	der Balletttänzer	derr bailet-tentser
ballet dancer (f)	die Balletttänzerin	dee bailet-tentserin
balloon	der Luftballon(s)	derr looft-ballon
banana	die Banane(n)	dee banane(r)
bandage	der Verband(¨e)	derr ferbant
bank river	das Ufer(-)	dass oofer
bank	die Bank(en)	dee bank
bank manager	der Geschäftsführer(-) der Bank	derr geshefts fewrer derr bank
barefoot	barfuß	barfooss
bargain	das Sonderangebot	dass zonder angeboat
to bark	bellen	betten
barn	die Scheune(n)	dee shoyne(r)
basement	das Untergeschoss(e)	dass oonter-geshoss
basket	der Korb(¨e)	derr korp
basket, shopping	der Einkaufskorb	drr yne-kowfs-korp
to have a bath	ein Bad nehmen	yne baht naymen
to run a bath	das Badewasser einlaufen lassen	dass bahde(r)-vasser yne-lowfen lassen
bathmat	die Bademstte(n)	dee bahde-matte(r)
bath robe	der Bademantel(¨)	derr bahde-mantle
bathroom	das Badezimmer(-)	dass bahde-tsimmer
bathtub	die Badewanne(n)	dee bahde-vanne(r)
to be	sein	zyne
to be born	geboren werden	geboren verden
to be called, to be named	heißen	hyssen
to be fond of	lieb haben	leep ha-ben
to be frozen	halb erfroren sein	halp erforen zyne
to be happy	glücklich sein	glewklikh zyne
to be hungry	Hunger haben	hoong-er ha-ben
to be late	zu spät kommen	tsoo shpyt kommen
to be on time	pünktlich sein	pewnkt-likh zyne
to be seasick	seekrank sein	zay-krank zyne
to be sick	sich übergeben	sikh owber-gayben
to sleepy	schläfrig sein	shlyvrikh zyne
to be thirsty	Durst haben	doorst ha-ben
beach	der Strand(¨e)	der shtrand
beak	der Schnabel(¨)	derr shna-bel
beans	die Bohnen (pl)	dee bonen
green bean	die Schnittbohne(n)	dee shnitt-bonen
beard	der Bart(¨e)	derr bart
to have a beard	einen Bart haben	ynen bart haben
bed	das Bett(en)	dass bet
to go to bed	ins Bett gehen	inss bet gayen
bedroom	das Schlafzimmer(-)	dass shlahf-tsimmer
bedside table	der Nachttisch(e)	derr nakht-tish
bedspread	die Tagesdecke(n)	dee dahgez-decke(r)
bedtime	die Schlafenszeit	dee shlahfens-tsyte
bee	die Biene(n)	dee beene(r)
beer	das Bier	dass beer
behind	hinter (acc or dat)	hinter
Belgium	Belgien	belg-yen
bell, doorbell	die Klingel(n)	dee kling-el
to belong, to be a member	Mitglied sein	mitgleed zyne
belt	der Gürtel(-)	derr gewrtel
safety belt, seatbelt	der Sicherheitsgurt(e)	derr zikher-hytes-goort
bench	Bank(¨e)	dee bank
beside	neben (acc or dat)	nayben
better	besser	besser
to feel better	sich besser fühlen	zich besser fewlen
between	zwischen (acc or dat)	tsvishen
beware of the dog!	Vorsicht bissiger Hund!	farzikht bissiger hoont
bicycle	das Fahrrad(¨er)	dass far-rat
big	groß	gross
bill	die Rechnung(en)	dee rekhnoong
bin	der Mülleimer(-)	derr mewl-ymer
biology	die Biologie	dee bee-ologee
bird	der Vogel (¨)	derr fogel
birth	die Geburt(en)	dee geboort
birthday	der Geburtstag(e)	derr geboorts-tag
birthday card	die (Geburtstags)Karte(n)	dee geboorts-tags-karte(r)
Happy birthday	Herzlichen Glückwunsch zum Geburtstag	herslikhen glewkvewnsh tsoom geboorts-tag
black	schwarz	shwarts
blackbird	die Amsel(n)	dee amsel
blackboard	die Tafel(n)	dee tahfel
block of apartments	der Wohnblock (s)	derr vone-block
blond	blond	blont
blond hair	blondes Haar(e)	blondes har
blouse	die Bluse(n)	dee blooze(r)
blue	blau	blaow
to board (ship or plane)	einsteigen	yne-shtygen
board game	dass Brettspiel(e)	dass brett-shpeel
boarding house	die Pension(en)	dee penzee-oan
boat	das Boot(e)	dass boat
to travel by boat	mit dem Schiff fahren	mit dehm shiff far-en
body	der Körper(-)	derr kewrpe(r)
book	das Buch(¨er)	dass bookh
picture book	das Bilderbuch(¨er)	dass Bilder-bookh
booked up, fully booked	belegt	belaygt
bookshop	der Buchladen(¨)	derr bookh-lahden
bookshop and stationer's	der Buchladen(¨) und die Schreibwarhung -handlung(en)	derr booklahden oont dee shrypvaren-handloong

110

boot (of car)	der Kofferraum(¨e)	derr kowfer-rowm
wellington boots	die Gummistiefel (pl)	dee-goomee-shteefel
boring	langweilig	langwyl-ig
to be born	geboren werden	geboren verden
boss (m)	der Chef(s)	derr chef
boss (f)	die Chefin(nen)	dee chefin
bottle	die Flasche(n)	dee flashe(r)
bouquet	der Blumenstrauß(¨e)	derr bloomen-shtrows
boutique	die Boutique(n)	dee boutique
bowl	die Suppentasse(n)	dee zoopen-tasse(r)
box office	die Kasse(n)	dee kasse(r)
boy	der Junge(n)	der yoong-e(r)
bra	der BH(s)	derr bay-ha
bracelet	das Armband(¨er)	dass arm-bant
to brake	bremsen	bremzen
branch	der Ast(¨e)	derr ast
brave	mutig	mootig
Bravo!	Encore!	oncore
bread	das Brot	dass broat
break (at school)	die Pause(n)	dee powze(r)
to break your leg	sich das Bein brechen	zikh dass byne brekhen
breakdown (vehicle)	die Panne(n)	dee panne(r)
to have a breakdown (vehicle)	eine Panne haben	yne panne haben
breakfast	das Frühstück(e)	dass frew-shtewk
to do breast-stroke	brustschwimmen	broost-shvimmen
bricklayer	der Maurer(-)	der maowrer
bride	die Braut(¨e)	dee browt
bridegroom	der Bräutigam(e)	derr browtigam
bridge	die Brücke(n)	dee brewke(r)
bright	leuchtend	loykhtend
to bring up	aufziehen	owf-tsee-en
broad	breit	brite
brooch	die Brosche(n)	dee broshe(r)
brother	der Bruder(¨)	derr brooder
brown	braun	brown
brown hair	braunes Haar (n)	brown-es har
bruise	der blaue Fleck(en)	derr blaowe fleck
brush (for painting)	der Pinsel(-)	derr pinzel
brush	die Bürste(n)	dee bewrste(r)
hairbrush	die Haarbürste(n)	dee hahr-bewrste(r)
toothbrush	die Zahnbürste(n)	dee tsahn-bewrste(r)
to brush your hair	sich die Haare bürsten	zikh dee hahre bewrst-en
Brussels sprouts	der Rosenkohl	deer rosen-cole
bucket	der Eimer(-)	derr eye-mer
buffet car	der Speisewagen(-)	derr shpyez(r)-vahgen
building	das Gebäude(-)	dass geboyde(r)
bulb (plant)	die Blumenzwiebel	dee bloomen-tsveebel
bunch of flowers	der Blumenstrauß(¨e)	derr bloomen-shtrowss
burn	die Verbrennung(en)	dee fer-brennoong
to burst out laughing	in Gelächter ausbrechen	in geleichter awssbrekhen
bus	der Bus(se)	derr booss
bus stop	die Bushaltestelle(n)	dee booshalte-stelle
to take the bus	mit dem Bus fahren	mit daym booss faren
bush	der Strauch(¨er)	derr shtrowkh
busy	beschäftigt	bee-sheftikt
bustling	belebt	be-laybt

butcher (or butcher's shop)	der Fleischer (-)	derr flysher
butter	die Butter	dee booter
buttercup	die Butterblume(n)	dee booter-bloome(r)
butterfly	der Schmetterling(e)	derr shmetterling
button	der Knopf(¨e)	derr knopf
to buy	kaufen	kowfen
by return mail	postwendend	post-vendend

C

cabbage	der Weißkohl	derr vyss-cole
cabin	die Kabine(n)	dee ka-beene(r)
cage	der Käfig(e)	derr kayfig
cake	die Torte(n)	dee torte(r)
cream cake	die Sahnetorte	dee zahne-torte(r)
cake shop	die Konditorei(en)	dee kondeeto-rye
to calculate	rechnen	rekhnen
calendar	Kalender(-)	derr kalender
calf	das Kalb(¨r)	dass kulp
camel	das Kamel(e)	dass kamayl
camera	die Kamera(s)	dee kamera
to camp, to go camping	zelten	tselten
camper	der Wohnwagen(-)	derr vone-vahgen
campsite	der Campingplatz(¨e)	derr camping-plats
can	die Dose(n)	dee doze(r)
Can I help you?	Womit kann ich dienen?	vo-mitt kan ikh deenen
Canada	Kanada	canada
candle	die Kerze(n)	dee kertse(r)
canned food	die Konserve(n)	dee conserve(r)
canoe	das Kanu(s)	dass kanoo
cap	die Mütze(n)	dee mewtse(r)
capital letter	der Großbuchstabe(n)	derr gross-bookh-shtabe(r)
to capsize	kentern	kentern
captain	der Kapitän(e)	derr kup-y-tayn
car	das Auto(s)	dass owto
car-park	der Parkplatz(¨e)	derr park-plats
card	die Karte(n)	dee karte(r)
credit card	die Kreditkarte(n)	dee kredit-karte(r)
postcard	die Postkarte(n)	dee post-karte(r)
card (playing cards)	die Karte(n)	dee karte(r)
to play cards	Karten spielen	karten shpeelen
cardigan	die Strickjacke(n)	dee shtrick-yacke(r)
careful	vorsichtig	for-zikhtig
careless	unvorsichtig	oon-for-zikhtig
caretaker (m)	der Hausmeister(-)	derr house-myster
caretaker (f)	die Hausmeisterin(nen)	dee house-mysterin
cargo	die Ladung(en)	dee la-doong
carpet	der Teppich(e)	derr teppikh
wall-to-wall carpet	der Teppichboden(¨)	derr teppikh-boden
carriage	der Wagen(-)	derr va-gen
to carry	tragen	tra-gen
carrot	die Karotte(n)	dee karotte(r)
cashier (m)	der Kassierer(-)	derr kasserer
cashier (f)	die Kassiererin(nen)	dee kasseerin
cassette	die Kassette(n)	dee kassette(r)
cassette recorder	der Kassettenrecorder(-)	derr kassetten-recorder
cat	die Katze(n)	dee katse(r)

111

to catch	fangen	fangen
to catch a fish	einen Fisch fangen	ybeb fish fangen
to catch a train	den Zug erreichen	dan tsug er-rykhen
cathedral	der Dom(e)	derr dome
cauliflower	der Blumenkohl	derr bloomen-coal
to celebrate	feiern	fy-ern
cellar	der Keller(-)	derr keller
cello	das Cello(-)	dass cello
to play the cello	Cello spielen	cello shpeelen
cemetery	der Friedhof(¨e)	freed-hofe
centimeter	der Zentimeter(-)	tsentimayter
chair	der Stuhl(¨e)	derr shdool
chairlift	der Sessellift(e)	derr zessel-lift
chalk	die Kreide(n)	dee kryder(r)
change (money)	das Kleingeld	dass klyn-gelt
Have you any small change?	Haben Sie Kleingeld?	ha-ben zee klyne-gelt
to change money	Geld wechseln	gelt vexeln
channel (TV and radio)	das Programm(e)	dass program
to chase	jagen	ya-gen
to chat	sich unterhalten	ziih ootler-halten
check-in	der Check-In	derr check-in
cheek	die Backe(n)	dee backe(r)
cheerful	fröhlich	fru(r)likh
cheese	der Käse(-)	derr kyze(r)
check	der Scheck(s)	derr sheck
to write a check	einen Scheck ausstellen	ynen sheck owss-shtellen
check-book	das Scheckbuch(¨er)	dass sheck-bookh
checkout	die Kasse(n)	dee kasse(r)
chemistry	die Chemie	dee khemee
cherry	die Kirsche(n)	dee kirshe(r)
to play chess	Schach spielen	shakh shpeelen
chest	die Brust(¨e)	dee broost
chicken	das Huhn(¨er)	dass hoon
child	das Kind(er)	dass kint
childhood	die Kindheit	dee kint-hyt
chimney	der Schornstein(e)	derr shorn-shtyn
chin	das Kinn(e)	dass kinn
China	China	kheena
chocolate	die Schokolade	dee shokolahde(r)
choir	der Chor(¨e)	der core
chop (meat)	das Kotelett(s)	dass kot-let
Christmas	Weihnachten	vy-nakhten
Christmas carol	das Weihnachtlied(er)	dass vy-nakhts-leed
Christmas Day	der erste Weihnachtstag	derr erste(r) vy-nakhts-tag
Christmas eve	der Heilige Abend	derr hylige(r) ahbend
Happy Christmas	Frohe Weihnachten	frohe(r) vynakhten
Christmas tree	der Weihnachtsbaum(¨e)	derr vynakthsbowm
church	die Kirche(n)	dee kirkhe(r)
circle	der Kreis	derr kryss
city	die Großstadt(¨e)	dee gross-shtat
to clap	klatschen	klatshen
classroom	das Klassenzimmer	dass klassentsimmer
claw	die Kralle(n)	dee kralle(r)
clean	sauber	zowber
to clean your teeth	sich die Zähne putzen	zikh dee tsyne(r) pootsen
climate	das Klima	dass kleema
to climb	klettern	klettern
to climb a tree	auf einen Baum klettern	aowf ynen baowm klettern
climber (m)	der Bergsteiger(-)	derr berg-shtyger
climber (f)	die Bergsteigerin(nen)	dee ber-shtygerin
clock	die Uhr(en)	dee our
alarm clock	der Wecker(-)	derr vecker
to close	zumachen	tsoo-makhen
clothes, clothing	die Oberbekleidung	dee obar-beklydoonk
clothes peg	die Wäscheklammer(n)	dee veshe(r)-klammer
cloud	die Wolke	dee volke(r)
coat	der Mantel(¨)	derr mantel
coatroom	die Garderobe(n)	dee garde(r)-robe(r)
cock	der Hahn(¨e)	derr hahn
cob	der Kabeljau(e)	derr kabel-yaow
coffee	der Kaffee	derr kaffay
coffee-pot	die Kaffeekanne(n)	dee kaffay-kanne(r)
coin	die Münze(n)	dee mewntse(r)
cold	kalt	kalt
It's cold.	Es ist kalt.	ess ist kalt
cold water	kaltes Wasser	kaltes vasser
to have a cold	eine Erkältung haben	yne(r) erkeltoong haben
to collect	sammeln	zammel
to collect stamps	Briefmarken sammeln	breef-marken zsammeln
collection	die Sammlung(en)	dee zamloong
collection, collection time	die Leerung(en)	dee layroong
color	die Farbe(n)	dee farbe(r)
colorful	bunt	boont
comb	der Kamm(¨e)	derr kamm
to comb your hair	sich die Haar kämmen	zikh dee hahre(r) kemmen
comic (book)	das Comic-Heft(e)	dass comic-heft
complexion	der Teint	derr te(n)
computer	der Computer(-)	derr computer
computer studies	die Informatik	dee informatik
conductor (orchestra) (m)	der Dirigent(en)	derr dirigent
conductor (f)	die Dirigentin(nen)	dee dirigentin
cone	der Kegel(n)	derr kaygel
to congratulate	gratulieren	gratoo-leeren
continent	der Erdteil	derr erd-tile
to cook	kochen	kokhen
cookie	der Keks(-)	der kecks
corner	die Ecke(n)	dee ecke(r)
to cost	kosten	kosten
It costs...	Das kostet...	dass kostet
cotton (made of cotton)	aus Baumwolle	owss bowm-volle(r)
counter	die Theke(n)	dee taeke(r)
country	das Land(¨er)	dass lant (dee lender)
countryside	das Land	dass lant
cousin (m)	der Vetter(n)	derr fetter
cousin (f)	die Kusine(n)	dee koozeene(r)
cow	die Kuh(¨e)	dee koo
cowshed	der Kuhstall(¨e)	derr koo-shtal
crab	der Krebs(e)	derr krayps
to crawl, to do the crawl	kraueln	krow-len
crayon	der Buntstift(e)	derr boont-shtift
cream	die Sahne	dee zahne(r)
cream cake	die Sahnetorte(n)	dee zahne(r)-tort(e)
credit card	die Kreditkarte	dee kredit-karte(r)
crew	die Besatzung(en)	dee bezatsoong
crib	das Kinderbett(en)	dass kinder-bet

cross, angry	böse	bu(r)ze(r)
to cross the street	die Straße überqueren	dee shtrasse(r) ewberkveren
crossing (sea)	die Überfahrt(en)	dee ewber-fart
crowd	die Menge	dee meng-e(r)
to cry	weinen	vynen
cup	die Tasse(n)	dee tasse(r)
cupboard	der Küchenschrank(¨e)	derr kewkhen-shrank
to cure	heilen	hylen
curly hair	Locken (pl)	locken
curtain	der Vorhang(¨e)	derr for-hang
customer (m)	der Kunde(m)	derr derr koonde(r)
customer (f)	die Kundin(nen)	dee koondin
customs	der Zoll	derr tsoll
customs officer (m)	der Zollbeamte(n)	derr tsoll-be(r)-amte(r)
customs officer (f)	die Zollbeamtin(nen)	dee tsoll-be(r)-amtin
cut (wound)	die Schnittwunde(n)	dee shnitt-voonde(r)

D

daffodil	die Osterglocke(n)	dee oaster-glocke(r)
dahlia	die Dahlie(n)	dee dal-ye(r)
daisy	das Gänseblümchen(-)	dass genze(r) blewmkhen
to dance	tanzen	tantsen
dance floor	die Tanzfläche(n)	dee tants-flekhe(r)
dark	dunkel	doornkel
dark (complexion)	braun	brown
It is dark.	Es ist dunkel.	ess ist dooonkel
It is getting dark.	Es wird dunkel.	ess veerrt doonkel
date	das Datum (pl: die Daten)	dass datoom (pl: dee da-ten)
daughter	die Tochter(¨)	dee tokhter
only daughter	die einzige Tochter	dee eyntsige(r) tokhter
dawn	das Morgengrauen(-)	dass morgen-graowen
day, daytime, in the daytime	der Tag(e)	derr tahg
the day after tomorrow	übermorgen	ewbermorgen
the day before yesterday	vorgestern	forgestern
Dear...	Lieber (m)/Liebe (f)	leeber/leebe(r)
Dear Sir/Madam	Sehr geehrte Damen und Herren	zayr ge(r)-rte(r) da-men oont herren
death	der Tod	der tot
December	Dezember	day-tzember
deck	das Deck(s)	das deck
deep	tief	teef
delicatessen	das Feinkostgeschäft(e)	das fine-kost-gesheft
delicious	lecker	lecker
to deliver	austeilen	owss-tylen
democratic	demokratisch	demokratish
dentist (m)	der Zahnarzt(¨e)	derr tsahn-artst
dentist (f)	die Zahnärztin(en)	dee tsahn-ertstin
department (in shop)	die Abteilung(en)	dee ap-tyloong
department store	das Kaufhaus (¨er)	dass kauf-house
Departures (in airport)	Abflug(¨e)	ap-floog
desert	die Wüste(n)	dee wowste(r)
designer (m)	der Designer(-)	derr designer
designer (f)	die Designerin(nen)	dee designer-in

dessert, pudding	die Nachspeise(n)/ das Dessert(s)	dee nakh-shpyze(r)/dass dessert
diary	der Kalender(-)	derr ka-lender
to die	sterben	shtarben
different	unterschiedlich	oonter-sheedlikh
difficult	schwierig	shveerig
to dig	graben	gra-ben
dining room	das Esszimmer(-)	dass ess-tsimmer
director	der Direktor(en)	derr direkt-or
dirty	schmutzig	shmootsig
disc jockey	der Diskjockey(s)	derr disc-jockey
discotheque	die Disko	dee Disko
to go to a discotheque	in die Disko gehen	in dee disco gayen
district	der Stadtteil(e)	derr shtat-tile
to dive	tauchen	taowkhen
to divide	teilen	tylen
divided by (maths)	geteilt durch	getylt doorkh
diving board	das Sprungbrett(er)	dass shproong-brett
to do	tun	toon
to do, to make	machen	makhen
to do back-stroke	rückenschwimmen	rewken-shvimmen
to do breast-stroke	brustschwimmen	broost-shvimmen
to do the dishes	abwaschen	ap-vashen
to do the gardening	im Garten arbeiten	im garten arbyten
docks, quay	der Kai(s)	derr kye
doctor (m)	der Arzt(¨e)	der artst
doctor (f)	die Ärztin(nen)	dee ertstin
dog	der Hund(e)	derr hoont
donkey	der Esel(-)	derr ayzel
door	die Tür(en)	dee tewr
front door	die Wohnungstür(en)	dee vo-noongs-tewr
doorbell	die Klingel(n)	dee kling-el
doormat	die Fußmatte(n)	dee foos-matte(r)
double room	das Doppelzimmer(-)	dass dopple-tsimmer
doughnut	der Berliner Pfannkuchen(-)	derr berliner pfann-kookhen
down	hinunter	hinoonter
downstairs	unten	oonten
to go downstairs	nach unten gehen	nakh oonten gayen
dragonfly	die Libelle(n)	dee libelle(r)
to play draughts	Dame spielen	da-me(r) shpeeln
to dream	träumen	troymen
dress	das Kleid(er)	dass klyde (dee klyde)
to get dressed	sich anziehen	sikh antsee-en
to drink	trinken	trinken
to drive	fahren	fahren
driver (m)	der Fahrer(-)	derr fahrer
driver (f)	die Fahrerin(nen)	dee fahrerin
to drop	fallen lassen	fa-len lassen
drums	das Schlagzeug(e)	dass shlag-tsoig
to play drums	Schlagzeug spielen	shlag-tsoig shpeelen
to dry, to wipe	abtrocknen	ap-trocknen
to dry your hair	sich die Haare fönen	zickh dee ha-re(r) fu(r)-nen
to dry yourself	sich abtrocknen	zich ap-trocknen
duck	die Ente(n)	dee ente(r)
dull	trüb	trewb
dungarees	die Latzhose(n)	dee lats-hoze(r)
duty-free shop	der Duty-free-Shop	der duty-free-shop

E

eagle	der Adler(-)	derr ahdler
ear	das Ohr(en)	dass ore
earring	der Ohrring(e)	derr ore-ring
east	der Osten	derr ost-en
Easter	Ostern	oastern
easy	einfach	yne-fakh
to eat	essen	essen
to have eaten well	gut gegessen haben	goot gegessen ha-ben
egg	das Ei(er)	das eye
eight	acht	akht
8 in the morning, 8 a.m.	acht Uhr morgens	akht oor morgens
8 in the evening, 8 p.m.	acht Uhr abends	akth oor ahbends
eighteen	achtzehn	akht-tsayn
eighty	achtzig	akht-tsig
elbow	der Ellbogen(-)	der ellbogen
election	die Wahl(en)	dee vahl
electricity	der Strom	derr shtrome
elephant	der Elefant(en)	derr ele-phant
elevator	der Aufzug(¨e)	derr owf-tsoog
eleven	elf	elf
emergency	der Notfall(¨e)	derr note-fal
emergency room	die Unfallsstation(en)	dee oonfal-shtatsion
to employ someone	jemanden einstellen	yaymanden yne-shtellen
employee (m)	der Angestellte(n)	derr an-ge(r)-shtellte(r)
employee (f)	die Angestellte(n)	dee an-ge(r)-shtellte(r)
empty	leer	layr
to empty	leeren	layren
Encore!	Zugabe!	tsoo-gahbe(r)
to get engaged	sich verloben	zsikh ferlohben
engine	die Lokomotive(n)	dee lokomoteeve(r)
English (language or subject)	Englisch	english
Enjoy your meal	Guten Appetit!	gooten appeteet
to enjoy yourself	sich gut unterhalten	zikh goot oonterhalten
to enjoy yourself, to have fun	Spaß haben	shpass ha-ben
enormous	riesig	reezig
entrance	der Eingang(¨e)	derr yne-gang
no entry (road)	keine Einfahrt	kyne yne-fart
envelope	der Umschlag(¨e)	derr oomshlag
Equator	der Äquator	derr ay-quator
escalator	die Rolltreppe(n)	dee roll-treppe(r)
Europe	Europa	oy-ropa
evening	der Abend(e)	derr ahbend
this evening	heute Abend	hoyte(r) ahbend
exam	die Prüfung(en)	dee prewfoong
to fail an exam	durchfallen	doorkh-fa-len
to pass an exam	bestehen	beshtyen
to sit an exam	eine Prüfung machen	eyne(r) prew-foong makhen
exchange rate	der Umtauschkurs(e)	derr oomtaowh-koors
to exercise	trainieren	tren-eeren
exercise book	das Heft(e)	dass heft
exhibition	die Ausstellung(en)	dee owss-shtelloong
exit	der Ausgang(¨e)	derr owss-gang
expensive	teuer	toyer
It's expensive.	Das ist teuer.	dass ist toyer
eye	das Auge(n)	dass owge(r)

F

fabric	der Stoff(e)	derr stoff
face	das Gesicht(er)	dass gzikht
factory	die Fabrik(en)	dee fabreek
to fail an exam	durchfallen	doorkh-fa-len
to faint	in Ohnmacht fallen	in oan-makht fa-len
fair	hellhäutig	hell-hoytig
fall (season)	der Herbst	derr herpst
to fall asleep	einschlafen	eyne-shlafen
false	falsch	falsh
family	die Familie(n)	dee fameel-ye(r)
famous	berühmt	berewmt
far	weit	vyte
far away from	weit weg von (dat)	vyte veck von
How far is...?	Wie weit ist...?	vee vyte ist
fare	der Fahrpreis(e)	derr fahr-price
farm	der Bauernhof(¨e)	derr baowern-hofe
farmer (m)	der Bauer(n)	derr baower
farmer (f), farmer's wife	die Bäuerin(nen)	dee boyerin
farmhouse	das Bauernhaus(¨er)	dass baowern-house
farmyard	der Hof(¨e)	derr hofe
fashionable	modisch	mo-dish
fast	schnell	shnell
fasten your seatbelts	bitte anschnallen	bette(r) an-shnal-en
fat	dick	dick
father	der Vater(¨)	derr fahter
feather	die Feder(n)	dee favder
February	Februar	febroo-ar
to feed	füttern	fewtern
to feel better	sich besser fühlen	zikh besser fewlen
to feel sick	sich krank fühlen	zikh krank fewlen
ferry	die Fähre(n)	dee feh-re(r)
to fetch	bringen	bringen
field	das Feld(en)	dass felt
fifteen	fünfzehn	fewnf-tsehn
the fifth (for dates only)	der, die, das fünfte	derr, dee, dass fewnfte(r)
fifty	fünfzig	fewnf-tsig
to fill	füllen	fewlen
to fill up with gas	volltanken	foll-tanken
to have a filling	sich einen Zahn plombieren	zikh eynen tsahn plombeeren
film	der Film(e)	der feelm
It's fine.	Es ist schön.	Ess ist shu(r)n
finger	der Finger(-)	derr fing-er
fire	das Feuer	dass foy-er
fire engine	das Feuerwehrauto(s)	dass foy-erfyr-owto
to fire someone	jemanden entlassen	yaymanden entlassen
fire station	die Feuerwache(n)	dee foyer vakhe(r)
fireman	der Feuerwehrmann(¨er)	derr foyer-vyr-man
fireplace	der Kamin(e)	derr kameen
the first	der, die, das erste	derr, dee, dass erst(r)
first class	die erste Klasse	dee erste(r) klase(r)
first floor	der erste Stock	derr erste(r)stock
first name	der Vorname(n)	derr for-nahme(r)
fish	der Fisch(e)	derr fish
to go fishing	zum Angeln gehen	tsoom ang-eln gayen

fishing boat	das Fischerboot(e)	dass fisher-boat
fishing red	die Angelrute(n)	dee ang-el-roote(r)
fishmonger	der Fischhändler	derr fish-hendler
to keep fit	fit halten	fit halten
five	fünf	fewnf
five past 10	fünf nach zehn	fewnf nakh tsyn
flag	die Flagge(n)	dee flagge(r)
flat tire	der Platte	derr platte(r)
flavor, taste	der Geschmack	derr geshmak
to float	treiben	try-ben
flock	die Herde(n)	dee herde(r)
flood	die Überschwem-mung(en)	dee ewbersh-vemmoong
floor	der Fußboden(")	derr fooss-boden
ground floor	das Erdgeschoss(e)	dass erd-geshoss
second floor	der zweite Stock	derr zsvyte(r) shtock
florist	das Blumengeschäft(e)	dass bloomen-gesheft
flour	das Mehl	dass mayl
flower	die Blume(n)	dee Bloome(r)
bunch of flowers	der Blumenstrauß(̈e)	derr bloomen-shtrows
flowerbed	das Blumenbeet(e)	dass bloomen-bayt
flowered (with flower pattern)	geblümt	geblewmt
fly	die Fliege(n)	die fleege(r)
to fly	fliegen	fleegen
fog	der Nebel	derr naybel
It's foggy.	Es ist neblig.	ess ist nayblig
to follow	verfolgen	ferfolgen
to be fond of	lieb haben	leep ha-ben
foot	der Fuß(̈e)	derr fooss
forget-me-not	das Vergissmeinnicht(-)	dass fergiss-mine-nikht
fork	die Gabel(n)	dee gahbel
form	das Formular(e)	dass formulahr
forty	vierzig	feertsig
forward	vorwärts	for-verts
foundation cream	das Make-up(s)	dass make-up
four	vier	feer
the fourth (for dates only)	der, die, das vierte	derr, dee, dass feerte(r)
fourteen	vierzehn	feer-tsayn
fox	der Fuchs(̈e)	derr fooks
fraction	der Bruch(̈e)	derr brookh
France	Frankreich	frank-rykh
freckles	die Sommersprossen (pl)	dee zommer-shprossen
freight train	der Güterzug(̈e)	derr gewter-tsoog
French (language or subject)	Französisch	fran-tseu(r)z-ish
fresh	frisch	frish
Friday	Freitag(m)	fry-tahg
fridge	der Kühlschrank(̈e)	derr kewl-shrank
friend (m)	der Freund(e)	derr froynt
friend (f)	die Freundin(nen)	dee fronydin
friendly	freundlich	froynt-likh
frightened	ängstlich	engst-likh
fringe	das Pony(s)	dass pony
frog	der Frosch(̈e)	derr frosh
front door	die Wohnungstür(en)	dee vo-noongs-tewr
to frown	die Stirn runzeln	dee shteern roontseln
frost	der Frost	derr frost
frozen food	die Tiefkühlkost	dee teef-kewl-kost
to be frozen	halb erfroren sein	halp erfroren zyne
fruit	das Obst	dass ohpst
fruit juice	der Fruchtsaft	derr frookht-zaft
full	voll	foll
full stop	der Punkt(e)	derr poonkt
fully booked	belegt	belaygt
fun	der Spaß	derr shpass
to have fun	Spaß haben	shpass ha-ben
funeral	die Beerdigung(en)	be(r)-erdigoong
funny	komisch	ko-mish
fur	das Fell	dass fell
furniture	die Möbel(pl)	dee mu(r)-bel
future	die Zukunft	dee tsookoonft
in the future	in der Zukunft	in derr tsookoonft

G

galaxy	die Milchstraße(n)	dee milk-shtrasse(r)
art gallery	die Kunstgalerie(n)	dee koonst-galeree
game	das Spiel(e)	dass shpeel
gangway	die Landungsbrücke(n)	dee landoongs-brewke
garage	die Garage(n)	dee ga-rahshe(r)
garbage collector	der Müllmann(̈er)	derr mewl-man
garden	der Garten(")	derr garten
garden shed	das Gartenhäuschen	dass garten-hors-khen
gardener (m)	der Gärtner(-)	derr gertner
gardener (f)	die Gärtnerin(nen)	dee gertnerin
to do the gardening	im Garten arbeiten	im garrten arbyten
garlic	der Knoblauch	derr k-no-blaowkh
gas	das Gas	dass gas
gas (fuel)	das Benzin	dass benzeen
gas station	die Tankstelle(n)	dee tank-shtelle(r)
to fill up with gas	volltanken	foll-tanken
gate	das Tor(e)	dass tore
to gather speed	schneller werden	shneller verden
generous	großzügig	gross-tsewgig
geography	die Erdkunde	dee erd-koonde(r)
geranium	die Geranie(n)	dee gerannee-ye
German (language or subject)	Deutsch	doytsh
Germany	Deutschland	doytsh-lant
to get dressed	sich anziehen	zich an-tsee-en
to get engaged	sich verloben	zich ferloben
to get married	heiraten	hye-raten
to get off (a bus or a train)	aussteigen	owss-shtygen
to get on	einsteigen	yne-shtygen
to get undressed	sich ausziehen	sikh owss-tsee-en
to get up	aufstehen	owf-stay-en
giraffe	die Giraffe(n)	dee giraffe(r)
girl	das Mädchen(-)	dass med-chen
to give	geben	gayben
to give (a present)	schenken	shenken
glass	das Glas(̈er)	dass glahss
glasses, pair of glasses	die Brille(n)	dee brille(r)
sunglasses	die Sonnenbrille(n)	dee zonnen-brille(r)
to wear glasses	eine Brille tragen	yne(r) brille(r) trahgen
glove	der Handschuh(e)	derr hant-shoe

to go	gehen	gay-en
to go to bed	ins Bett gehen	inss bet gay-en
to go downstairs	nach unten gehen	nakh oonten gay-en
to go fishing	zum Angeln gehen	tsoom ang-eln gay-en
to go on holiday	in Urlaub fahren	in oorlaowp fa-ren
to go mountaineering	zum Bergsteigen gehen	tsoom berg-shtygen gay-en
to go to the movies	ins Kino gehen	inss keeno gay-en
to go upstairs	nach oben gehen	nakh oben gay-en
to go for a walk	spazieren gehen	shpatseeren gay-en
to go window-shopping	einen Schaufenster-bummel machen	eynen shaowf-fenster boomel makhen
to go to work	zur Arbeit gehen	tsoor arbyte gay-en
goal	das Tor(e)	dass tore
goalkeeper	der Torwart(e)	derr tore-vart
goat	die Ziege(n)	dee tseege(r)
gold	das Gold	dass golt
made of gold	aus Gold	owss golt
goldfish	der Goldfisch(e)	derr golt-fish
goldfish bowl	das Goldfischglas(¨er)	dass golt-fish-glahss
golf club	der Golfschläger(-)	derr golf-shlager
to play golf	Golf spielen	golf speelen
good	gut	goot
Good luck!	Viel Glück.	feel glewk
Good morning	Guten Morgen	gooten morgen
good value	preiswert	price-vert
It's good value.	Das ist preiswert.	dass ist price-vert
It tastes good.	Das schmeckt gut.	dass shmeckt goot
Goodbye	Auf Wiedersehen	owf veeder-zay-en
Goodbye (on telephone)	Wiederhören	veeder-huren
Good night	Gute Nacht	goote nakhd
goose	die Gans(¨e)	dee ganss
gorilla	der Gorilla(s)	derr gorila
government	die Regierung(en)	dee regeeroong
grain	das Getreide	dass getryde(r)
grammar	die Grammatik	dee gram-atik
granddaughter	die Enkelin(nen)	dee eknelin
grandfather	der Großvater(¨)	derr gross-fahter
grandmother	die Großmutter(¨)	dee gross-mooter
grandson	der Enkel(-)	derr enkel
grape	die Weintraube(n)	dee vine-trowbe(r)
grass	das Gras	dass grahss
gray	grau	graow
Great Britain	Großbritannien	gross britannien
green	grün	grewn
greenhouse	das Gewächshaus(¨er)	dass gevecks-house
grocery shop	das Lebensmittel geschäft(e)	dass laybens-mittel-gesheft
ground floor	das Erdgeschoss(e)	dass erd-geshoss
to growl	knurren	knooren
guard	der Schaffner	derr shaffner
guest (m)	der Gast(¨e)	der gast
guest house, boarding house	die Pension(en)	dee penz-ion
guinea pig	das Meerschweinchen(-)	dass mayr-shvine-khen

guitar	die Gitarre(n)	dee gitarre(r)
to play the guitar	Gitarre spielen	gitarre(r) shpeelen
gymnastics	die Gymnastik	dee gem-nastik
gym shoes	die Turnschuhe (pl)	dee toorn-sho-e(r)

H

hail	der Hagel	derr hahgel
to hail a taxi	ein Taxi rufen	yne taxi roofen
hair	das Haar(e)	dass har
to have (...) color hair	(...) Haar haben	... har ha-ben
hairdresser (m), hairdresser's	der Friseur(e)	derr frizz-er
hairdresser (f), hairdresser's	die Friseurin(nen)	dee frizz-ewrin
hair-drier	der Fön(s)	derr fo(r)n
a half	die Hälfte(n)	dee helfte(r)
half a kilo	ein Pfund(e)	yne pfoont
half a liter	ein halber Liter(-)	yne halber litre
half past 10	halb elf	halp elf
half slip	der Halbunterrock(¨e)	derr halp-unter rock
ham	der Schinken(-)	derr shinken
hammer	der Hammer(¨)	derr hammer
hamster	der Hamster(-)	derr hamster
hand	die Hand(¨e)	dee hant
handbag	die Handtasche(n)	dee hant-tashe(r)
hand luggage	das Handgepäck	dass hant-gepeck
handsome	gutaussehend	goot ows-zayend
to hang on to	sich festhalten an	zikh fest hal-ten an
to hang up (telephone)	auflegen	owf-laygen
happy	glücklich	glewk-likh
to be happy	glücklich sein	glewk-likh zyne
Happy birthday	Herzlichen Glückwunsch zum Geburtstag	hertszlikhen glewk-voonsh tsoom geboorts-tahg
Happy New Year	Glückliches Neues Jahr	glewklikhes noyes yar
hard	hart	hart
hard-working	fleißig	fly-sig
to harvest	ernten	ernten
hat	der Hut(¨e)	derr hoot
Have you any small change?	Haben Sie Kleingeld?	ha-ben zee klyne-gelt
to have	haben	ha-ben
to have a bath	ein Bad nehmen	yne baht naymen
to have a break-down (vehicle)	eine Panne haben	yne panne(r) ha-ben
to have a cold	eine Erkältung haben	yne erkeltoong ha-ben
to have a filling	sich einen Zahn plombieren lassen	zickh ynen tsahn plom-bieeeren lassen
to have a flat tire	einen Platten haben	ynen platen ha-ben
to have fun	Spaß haben	shpass ha-ben
to have a showder	duschen	dooshen
to have stomach ache	Bauchweh haben	baowkh-vay ha-ben
to have a temperature	Fieber haben	feeber ha-ben
to have toothache	Zahnschmerzen haben	tsahn shmert-sen ha-ben

Having a lovely time.	Es ist ganz toll hier.	ess ist gants toll here
hay	das Heu	dass hoy
haystack	der Hauhaufen(-)	derr hoy-howfen
head	der Kopf(¨e)	derr kopf
to have a headache	Kopfschmerzen haben	kopf-shmertsen ha-ben
headband	das Stirnbank(¨er)	dass shteeribant
headlight	der Scheinwerfer(-)	derr shine-verfer
headline	die Schlagzeile(n)	dee shlag-tsyle(r)
headmistress	die Direktorin(nen)	dee direkt-orin
headphones	die Köpfhörer (pl)	dee kuhpf-hu)r)-rer
healthy	gesund	gezoont
heavy	schwer	shver
to be heavy	schwer sein	shver zyne
hedgehog	der Igel(-)	derr eegel
heel	die Ferse(n)	dee ferze(r)
height	die Größe	dee gru(r)sse(r)
Hello	Hallo	hallo
to help	helfen	helfen
Help yourself!	Greif zu.	grife tsoo
Can I help you?	Womit kann ich dienen?	vo-mit kan ikh deenen
henhouse	der Hühnerstall(¨e)	derr hewner-shtal
herbs	die Kräuter (pl)	dee kryter
hero	der Held(en)	derr helt
heroine	die Heldin(nen)	dee heldin
herring	der Hering(e)	derr hayring
to hide	sich verstecken	zikh verstecken
hill	der Hügel(-)	derr hewgel
hippopotamus	das Nilpferd(e)	dass neel-pfert
His name is...	Er heißt...	er hysst
history	die Geschichte	dee geshikhte(r)
hold (ships)	der Laderaum(¨e)	derr lahde(r)-raowm
to hold	halten	hal-ten
honey	der Honig	derr ho-nig
honeymoon	die Flitterwochen (pl)	dee flitter-vokhen
hood (car)	die Motorhaube(n)	dee motor-howbe(r)
hook (for fishing)	der Angelhaken(-)	derr ang-el haken
horn	die Hupe(n)	dee hoope(r)
horse	das Pferd(e)	dass pfert
horse racing	das Pferderennen(-)	dass pferde(r)-rennen
hospital	das Krankenhaus(¨er)	dass kranken-house
hot	heiß	hyss
hot water	heißes Wasser	hysses vasser
I'm hot.	Mir ist warm.	meer ist varm
hotel	das Hotel(s)	dass hotel
to stay in a hotel	im Hotel wohnen	im hotel vo-nen
hour	die Stunde(n)	dee stoonde(r)
house	das Haus(¨er)	dass hows
How are you?	Wie geht's?	vee gayts
How far is...?	Wie weit ist...?	vee vyte ist
how much..?	wie viel..?	vee feel
How much is...?	Was kostet...?	vass kostet
How much is that?	Wie viel macht das?	vee feel makht das
How old are you?	Wie alt bist du?	vee alt bist doo
hump (camel's)	der Höcker(-)	derr hu(r)ker
hundred	hundert	hoondert
to be hungry	Hunger haben	hoong-er ha-ben
husband	der Ehemann(¨er)	derr aye(r)-man

I

I agree.	Das meine ich auch.	dass myne(r) ikh owkh
I am sending ... separately	Mit getrennter Post erhältst du...	mit getrennter post erhelst doo
I enclose (...)	Beigefügt finden Sie (...)	by-gefu(r)gt finden zee
I'll call you back. (on telephone)	Ich rufe dich zurück.	ikh roofe(r) dikh zoorewk
I would like...	Ich hätte gern...	ikh hette gern
I'm nineteen.	Ich bin neunzehn.	ikh bin noyn-tsayn
ice-cream	das Eis	dass ice
icicle	der Eiszapfen	derr ice-tsapfen
sick	krank	krank
to feel sick	sich krank fühlen	zikh krankh fewlen
important	wichtig	vikh-tig
in (for sports)	nicht aus	nikht ows
in	in (dat)	in
in focus	scharf	sharf
in front of	vor (dat or acc)	for
in the future	in der Zukunft	in derr tsookoonft
India	Indien	indien
indicator	der Blinker(-)	derr blinker
ingredient	die Zutat(en)	dee tsoo-tat
injection	die Spritze(n)	dee shpritse(r)
instrument	das Instrument(e)	das instru-ment
inter-city-train	der Intercity	derr intercity
interesting	interessant	interess-ant
to interview	interviewen	interviewen
into	in (acc)	in
to introduce	vorstellen	for-shtellen
to invite	einladen	yne-laden
to iron	bügeln	bewgln
Is service included?	Mit Bedienung?	mit bedeenoong
It costs...	Das kostet...	dass kostet
It is getting light.	Es wird hell.	ess veert hell
It is light.	Es ist hell.	es ist hell
It is 1 o'clock.	Es ist ein Uhr.	ess ist yne oor
It is 3 o'clock.	Es ist drei Uhr.	ess ist drye oor
It's... (on phone)	Hier ist...	here ist
It's cold.	Es ist kalt.	ess ist kalt
It's fine.	Es ist schön.	ess ist shawn
It's foggy.	Es ist neblig.	ess ist nayblig
It's good value.	Es ist preiswert.	ess ist price-vert
It's raining.	Es regnet.	ess raygnet
It's ready. (for meal)	Das Essen ist fertig.	dass essen ist fertig
It's snowing.	Es schneit.	ess schnyte
It's windy.	Es ist windig.	ess ist vindig
It was lovely to hear from you.	Schön, mal wieder von dir zu hören.	sho(r)n, mal veeder fon deer tsoo ho(r)-ren
Italy	Italien	italien

J

jacket	die Jacke(n)	dee yacke(r)
jam	die Marmelade(n)	dee marme(r)-lade(r)
Japan	Japan	yapan
jeans	die Jeans (pl)	dee jeans
jewelry	der Schmuck	derr shmook
job, profession	der Beruf(e)	derr beroof
to jog	joggen	yoggen

to join	Mitglied werden	mit-gleed verden
joint, roast	der Braten	derr brahten
journalist (m)	der Journalist(en)	derr journaleest
journalist (f)	die Journalistin(nen)	dee jounrna-leestin
judge (m)	der Richter(-)	derr rikhter
judge (f)	die Richterin(en)	dee rikhterin
juice	der Safte(¨e)	derr zaft
fruit juice	der Fruchtsaft(¨e)	derr frookht-zaft
July	Juli	yulee
June	Juni	yunee
jungle	der Dschungel(-)	derr djoongel

K

kangaroo	das Känguruh(s)	dass kengooroo
to keep an eye on	aufpassen auf	owf-pasen owf
to keep fit	fit halten	fit halten
kennel	die Hundehütte(n)	dee hoonde(r)-hewte(r)
keyboard	die Tastatur(en)	dee tass-ta-toor
kilo	das Kilo(-)	dass keelo
A kilo of...	Ein Kilo...	yne keelo
Half a kilo of...	Ein Pfund...	yne pfoont
to kiss	küssen	kewsen
kitchen	die Küche(n)	dee kewkhe(r)
kitten	das Kätzchen(-)	dass ktes-khen
knee	das Knie(-)	dass k-nee
to kneel down	sich hinknien	sikz hin-k-nee-en
to be kneeling	knien	k-nee-en
knife	das Messer(-)	dass messer
to knit	stricken	shtricken
knitting needles	die Stricknadeln (pl)	dee shtrick-nadeln
to knock over	umwerfen	oom-verfen

L

label	ein Anhänger(-)	yne an-hen-ger
ladder	die Leiter(-)	dee lyter
lake	der See(n)	derr zay
lamb	das Lamm(¨er)	dass lamb
lamp	die Lampe(n)	dee lampe(r)
to land	landen	landen
landlady	die Eigentümerin(nen)	dee eygen-tewmerin
landlord	der Eigentümer(-)	derr eygen-tewmer
landscape	die Landschaft(en)	dee lantshaft
large (clothes size)	groß	gross
last	letzte	letste(r)
late	verspätet	fer-shpaytet
to be late	zu spät kommen	tsoo shpayt kommen
to laugh	lachen	lakhen
to burst out laughing	in Gelächter ausbrechen	in glekhder ows-brekhen
lawn	der Rasen(-)	derr rahzen
lawnmower	der Rasenmäher(-)	derr rahzen-mayer
lawyer (m)	der Rechtsanwalt(¨e)	derr rekhts-anvalt
lawyer (f)	die Rechtsanwältin(nen)	dee rekhts-anvaltin
to lay eggs	Eier legen	eyer legen
to lay the table	den Tisch decken	den tishdecken
lazy	faul	fowl
leader (m/f)	der/die Vorsitzende(r)	derr/dee for-zitsende(r)
leaf	das Blatt(¨er)	das blatt
to lean on	lehnen an	laynen an

to learn	lernen	lernen
left luggage office	die Gepäckaufbewahrung	dee gepeck-owfbevahroon
left, left side	die linke Seite	dee linke(r) zyte(r)
on the left, left wing	links	links
leg	das Bein(e)	dass bine
lemon	die Zitrone(en)	dee tsitrone(r)
lentils	die Linsen (pl)	dee linzen
length	die Länge(n)	dee lenge(r)
lesson	die Unterrichtsstunde(n)	dee oonter-rikhts-shtoonde(r)
letter	der Brief(e)	derr brief
letter of alphabet	der Buchstabe(n)	derr bookh-shtahbe
letter box	der Briefkasten(¨)	derr brief-kasten
liberal (politics)	liberal	liberal
library	die Bücherei(en)	dee bewkher-eye
license plate	das Nummernschild(er)	dass noomern-shilt
to lie down	sich hinlegen	zikh hin-laygen
life	das Leben	dass layben
lifeguard	der Rettungs-schwimmer(-)	derr rettoongs-shvimmer
light (weight)	leicht	lykht
to be light (weight)	leicht sein	lykht zine
light (lamp)	die Lampe(n)	dee lampe(r)
It is light.	Es ist hell.	ess ist hell
It is getting light.	Es wird hell.	ess veert hell
lightning	der Blitz(e)	derr blitz
to line up	anstehen	an-shtayen
liner	das Passagierschiff(e)	dass passageer-shiff
lion	der Löwe(n)	derr lo(r)ve(r)
lip	die Lippe(n)	dee lippe(r)
lipstick	der Lippenstift(e)	derr lippen-shtift
list	die Liste(n)	dee liste(r)
to make a list	eine Liste machen	yne(r) liste(r) makhen
to listen	hören	ho(r)-en
to listen to music	Musik hören	moozeek ho(r)-en
to listen to radio	Radio hören	ra-dio ho(r)-en
liter	der Liter(-)	derr leeter
half a liter	ein halber Liter(-)	yne halber leeter
to live	wohnen	vo-nen
to live in a house	in einem Haus wohnen	in ynem house vo-nen
lively	lebhaft	layb-haft
living room	das Wohnzimmer(-)	dass vone-tsimmer
to load	laden	la-den
loaf	der Laib(e)	derr lybe
long	lang	lang
to look for	suchen	zukhen
loose	weit	vyte
to lose	verlieren	fer-leeren
loudspeaker	der Lautsprecher(-)	derr laowt-shprekher
Love from... (end of letter)	Alles Gute...	al-ez goote(r)
to love	lieben	leeben
luck	das Glück	dass glewk
Good luck	Viel Glück	feel glewk
luggage cart	der Gepäckwagen(-)	derr gepeck-vahgen
luggage-rack	die Gepäckablage(n)	dee gepeck-ap-lahge(r)
lullaby	das Schlaflied(er)	dass shlahf-leet
lunch	das Mittagessen(n)	dass mittag-essen

lunch hour	die Mittagspause(n)	dee mittags-powze(r)
to be lying down	liegen	leegen

M

made of metal	aus Metall	owss metall
made of plastic	aus Plastik	owss pla-stick
magazine	die Zeitschrift(en)	dee tsyte-shrift
airmail	Luftpost	looft-post
mail-box	der Briefkasten(¨)	derr brief-kasten
main course	das Hauptgericht(e)	dass howpt-gerikht
main road	die Hauptstraße(n)	dee howpt-strasse(r)
to make	machen	makhen
to make a list	eine Listen machen	yne(r) liste makhen
to make a phonecall	telefonieren	telephoneeren
to make, to build	bauen	bow-en
to put on make-up	sich schminken	zikh shminken
man	der Mann(¨er)	der man
map	die Karte(n)	dee karte(r)
March	März	merts
margarine	die Margarine	dee mar-ga-reene(r)
market	der Markt(¨e)	derr markrt
market place	der Marktplatz(¨e)	derr markt-plats
to shop at the market	auf dem Markt einkaufen	owf daym markt yne-kowfen
market stall	der Marktstand(¨e)	derr markt-stant
marriage	die Ehe(n)	dee aye(r)
to get married	heiraten	hye-raten
mascara	die Wimperntusche(n)	dee vimpern-tooshe(r)
maths	Mathematik	matema-tick
May	Mai	mey
meadow	die Wiese(n)	dee veese(r)
measure	messen	messen
meat	das Fleisch	dass flysh
mechanic (m)	der Automechaniker(-)	derr owto-mekhaniker
the media	die Medien (pl)	dee maydien
medium (clothes)	mittel	mittell
to meet	treffen	treffen
melon	die Melone(n)	dee melone(r)
member (m/f)	das Mitglied (er)	dass mit-gleet
member of parliament (m/f)	der/die Abgeordnete(n)	derr/dee apge(r) ordnete(n)
to mend	reparieren	repareeren
to mend (clothing)	flicken	flicken
menu	die Speisekarte(n)	dee shpyze-kart(r)
merry-go-round	das Karussell(e)	dass caroosel
metal	das Metall(e)	dass metall
made of metal	aus Metall	ows metall
meter	der Meter(-)	derr mayter
to mew	miauen	miaw-en
midday	Mittag	mitag
midnight	Mitternacht	mitter-nakht
milk	die Milch	dee milkh
to milk	melken	melken
a million	eine Million	yne(r) mill-yon
mineral water	das Mineralwasser	dass miner-al-vasser
minus (maths)	weniger	vayniger
mirror	der Spiegel(-)	derr shpeegel
miserable	schlecht gelaunt	shlekht gelaownt
to miss the train	den Zug verpassen	dayn tsoog fer-passen
to mix	rühren	rewren
model (m/f)	das Mannequin(s)	dass manay-kin

mole	der Maulwurf(¨e)	derr mowl-worf
Monday	Montag(e)	mon-tag
money	das Geld	dass gelt
to change money	Geld wechseln	gelt veckseln
to put money in the bank, to pay money in	Geld einzahlen	gelt yne-tsahlen
to take money out	Geld abheben	gelt ap-hayben
monkey	der Affe(n)	derr affe(r)
month	der Monat(e)	derr mo-nat
moon	der Mond	derr moant
moped	das Moped(s)	dass moped
morning	der Morgen(-)	derr morgen
8 in the morning, 8 a.m.	acht Uhr morgens	akht oor morgens
this morning	heute Morgen	hoyte(r) morgen
mosquito	die Mücke(n)	dee mewke(r)
mother	die Mutter(¨)	dee mooter
motor racing	das Autorennen(-)	dass owto-rennen
motorbike	das Motorrad(¨er)	dass mo-to-rad
mountain	der Berg(e)	derr berg
mountaineering	das Bergsteigen	dass berg-shtygen
to go mountaineering	zum Bergsteigen gehen	tsoom berg-stygen gay-en
mouse	die Maus(¨e)	dee mouse
moustache	der Schnurrbart(¨e)	derr shnoorbart
to have a moustache	einen Schnurrbart haben	ynen shnoorbart ha-ben
mouth	der Mund(¨er)	derr moont
to move in	einziehen	yne-tsee-en
to move out	ausziehen	owss-tsee-en
movies	das Kino(s)	dass keeno
to go to the movies	ins Kino gehen	inss keeno gayen
to mow the lawn	den Rasen mähen	dayn ra-zen mayen
to multiply	malnehmen	mal-naymen
music	die Musik(en)	dee moozeek
classical music	die klassische Musik	dee klassishe(r) moozeek
pop music	die Popmusik	dee pop-moozeek
musician (m)	der Musiker(-)	derr mooziker
musician (f)	die Musikerin(nen)	dee moozikerin
mussel	die Muscheln (pl)	deemossheln
mustard	der Senf	derr zenf
My name is...	Ich heiße...	ikh hysse(r)

N

naked	nackt	nackt
name	der Name(n)	derr na-me(r)
first name	der Vorname(n)	derr for-na-me(r)
surname	der Nachname(n)	derr nakh-na-me(r)
His name is...	Er heißt...	er hysst
My name is...	Ich heiße...	ikh hysse
What's your name?	Wie heißt du?	vee hysst doo
napkin	die Serviette(n)	dee serv-iette(n)
narrow	schmal	shmal
naughty	frech	frekh
navy blue	marineblau	marine(r)-blaow
near	nahe an (dat)	nahe(r) an
neck	der Hals(¨e)	derr halss
necklace	die Halskette(n)	dee halss-kette(n)
needle	die Nadel(n)	dee na-del
needlework and yarn shop	das Handarbeits-geschäft(e)	dass hant-arbyts-gesheft
neighbor (m)	der Nachbar(n)	derr nakhbar
neighbor (f)	die Nachbarin(nen)	dee nakhbarin

nephew	der Neffe(n)	derr neffe(r)
nest	das Nest(er)	dass nest
net (tennis court)	dass Netz(e)	dass nets
net (fishing)	das Netz(e)	dass nets
Netherlands	die Niederlande (pl)	dee needer-lande(r)
new	neu	noy
New Year's Day	Neujahr	noy-yar
New Year's Eve	Silvester	zilvester
Happy New Year	Glückliches Neues Jahr	glewk-likhes noyez yar
New Zealand	Neuseeland	noy-zaylant
news	die Nachrichten (pl)	dee nakh-rikhten
newspaper	die Zeitung(en)	dee tsyte-oong
newspaper stand	der Kiosk(e)	derr kiosk
next	nächste	nexte(r)
the next day	am nächsten Tag	am nexten tahg
next Monday	nächsten Montag	nexten moan-tahg
next week	nächste Woche	nexte(r) vokhe(r)
niece	die Nichte(n)	dee nikhte(r)
night	die Nacht(ˉe)	dee nakht
nightgown	das Nachthemd(en)	dass nakht-hemt
nine	neun	noyn
911 call	der Notruf(e)	derr note-roof
nineteen	neunzehn	noyn-tsayn
ninety	neunzig	noyn-tsig
no	nein	nine
no entry (road sign)	keine Einfahrt	kyne yne-fart
no parking	Parkverbot	park ferboat
no smoking	Nichtraucher	nikht-rowkher
noise	laut	lauwt
noodles	die Nudeln (pl)	dee noodeln
north	der Norden	derr norden
North Pole	der Nordpol	derr nord-pole
nose	die Nase(n)	dee naze(r)
nothing	nichts	nikhts
Nothing to declare	Nicht zu verzollen	nikhts tsoo fer-tsollen
novel	der Roman(e)	derr ro-man
November	November	november
now, nowadays	jetzt	jetst
nurse (m)	der Krankrenpfleger	derr kranken-pflayger
nurse (f)	die Krankenschwester	dee kranken-shvester

O

oak tree	die Eiche(n)	dee ykhe(r)
oar	das Ruder	dass rooder
obedient	gehorsam	gehorzam
It is one o'clock.	Es ist ein Uhr.	ess ist yne oor
It is 3 o'clock.	Es ist drei Uhr.	ess ist dry oor
October	Oktober	october
odd jobs	das Heimwerken	dass hyme-verken
office	das Büro(s)	dass bewro
offices, office block	das Bürogebäude	dass bewro-geboyde(r)
oil (engine food)	das Öl	dass o(r)l
old	alt	alt
old-fashioned	altmodisch	alt-modish
old age	das Alter	dass alt-er
older than	älter als	elter alss
on	auf (acc or dat)	aowf
on time	pünktlich	pewnkt-likh
one	eins	ynss
onion	die Zwiebel(n)	dee tsveebel
open	offen	offen
to open	öffnen	o(r)fnen

to open a letter	einen Brief öffnen	ynen brief o(r)fnen
to open the curtains	die Vorhänge aufziehen	dee foreheng(r) owf-tsee-en
opera	die Oper(n)	dee o-per
operating theatre	der Operationssaal	derr operatsee-onz-zahl
operation	die Operation(en)	dee operatsee-oan
orange (color)	orange	o-range(r)
orange (fruit)	die Apfelsine(n)	dee apfel-zeene(r)
orchard	der Obstgarten(ˉ)	derr oapst-garten
orchestra	das Orchester(-)	dass orkester
to order	bestellen	be-shtellen
ostrich	der Strauß	derr shtrowss
out (for sports)	aus	owss
out of	aus (dat)	owss
out of focus	unscharf	oon-sharf
oven	der Backofen(ˉ)	derr back-oafen
over	über (acc or dat)	ewber
overtime	Überstunden (pl)	ewber-shtoonden
owl	die Eule(n)	dee oyle(r)

P

Pacific Ocean	der Pazifik	derr pa-tsifeek
to pack	packen	packen
package	das Paket(e)	das pa-keyt
packet	das Päckchen	dass peck-khen
to paddle	planschen	plan-shen
paint	die Farbe(n)	dee farbe(r)
to paint	malen	ma-len
painter (m)	der Künstler(-)	derr kewnstler
painter (f)	die Künstlerin(nen)	dee kewnstleren
painting	das Gemälde(-)	dass gemelde(r)
pale	blass	blass
pants	die Hose(n)	dee hoze(r)
paper	das Papier	dass papeer
paperback	das Taschenbuch(ˉ)	dass tashen-bookh
paper money	die Banknote(n)	dee banknote(r)
parents	die Eltern (pl)	dee eltern
park	der Park(s)	derr park
park keeper	der Parkwächter(-)	der park-vekhter
to park	parken	parken
no parking	Parkverbot	park-ferbote
parliament	das Parlament(e)	dass parlament
parrot	der Wellensittich(e)	derr vellen-zittikh
party (celebration)	die Party(s)	dee party
party (political)	die Partei(en)	dee part-eye
to pass an exam	bestehen	be(r)-shtayen
to pass (in car)	überholen	ewber-holen
passenger (m/f)	der Pasagier(e)	derr passajeer
passport	der Pass(ˉe)	derr pass/dee pesse(r)
past	die Vergangenheit	dee fer-gangenhyte
pastry, Danish	der Hefekuchen(-)	derr hayfe(r)-ko(e)-khen
pastry		
path	der Weg(e)	derr vayg
path, country lane	der Pfad(e)	derr pfaht
patient (m)	der Patient(en)	derr pats-yent
patient (f)	die Patientin(nen)	dee pats-yentin
pattern	das Muster(-)	das mooster
paw	die Pfote(n)	dee pfote(r)
PE	der Sport	derr shport
pea	die Erbse(n)	dee erpse(r)
peaceful	friedlich	freed-likh

peach	die Pfirsich(e)	dee pfirzikh
pear	die Birne(n)	dee beerne(r)
pedestrian (m)	der Fußgänger(-)	derr fooss-genger
pedestrian (f)	die Fußgängerin(nen)	dee fooss-gengereen
pedestrian crossing	der Zebrastreifen(-)	derr zebra-shtryfen
pen	der Füller(-)	derr fewler
ball-point	der Kugelschreiber(-)	derr koogel-shryber
pencil	der Bleistift	derr bly-shtift
pencilcase	das Etui(s)	dass ay-twee
penguin	der Pinguin(e)	derr pingooin
pepper	der Pfeffer	derr pfeffer
to perch	hocken	hocken
to perform, to appear on stage	auftreten	owf-trayten
perfume	das Parfüm(s)	dass parfume
petticoat, slip	der Unterrock(¨e)	derr oonter-rock
pharmacy	die Drogerie(n)	dee drogeree
photograph	das Foto(s)	dass photo
to take a photo	ein Foto machen	yne photo makhen
photographer (m)	der Fotograf(en)	derr photograph
photographer (f)	die Fotografin(nen)	dee photographin
photography	die Fotografie(n)	dee photographee
physics	die Physik	dee phewzick
piano	das Klavier(e)	dass klaveer
to play the piano	Klavier spielen	klaveer shpeelen
to pick	pflücken	pflewken
to pick flowers	Blumen pflücken	bloomen pflewken
to pick up	aufheben	owf-hayben
to pick up the receiver	den Telefonhörer abheben	den telephon-ho(r)er apnaymen
picnic	das Picknick	dass picnic
pig	das Schwein(e)	dass shvine
pigeon	die Taube(n)	dee taowebe(r)
pill	die Tablett(en)	dee tablette(r)
pillow	das Kopfkissen	dass kopf-kissen
pilot (m)	der Pilot(en)	derr pee-lote
pilot (f)	die Pilotin(nen)	dee pee-lotin
pin	die Stecknadel(n)	dee shteck-nahdel
pine tree	die Tanne(n)	dee tanne(r)
pink	rosa	roza
sports field	der Sportplatz(¨e)	derr shport-plats
to pitch a tent	ein Zelt aufbauen	yne tselt owf-bowen
pitcher	der Krug(¨e)	derr kroog
plaice	die Scholle(n)	dee sholle(r)
to plant	pflanzen	pflantsen
plastic	das Plastik	dass plastic
made of plastic	aus Plastik	ows plastic
plate	der Teller	derr teller
platform	der Bahnsteig(e)	derr bahn-shteyk
platform ticket	die Bahnsteigkarte(n)	dee bahn-shtyk-karte(r)
play (theatre)	das Stück(e)	dass shtewk
to play (to play an instrument)	spielen	shpeelen
to play cards	Karten spielen	karten shpeelen
to play chess	Schach spielen	shakh shpeelen
to play draughts	Dame spielen	dahme(r) shpeelen
to play golf	Golf spielen	golf shpeelen
to play squash	Squash spielen	sqash shpeelen
to play tennis	Tennis spielen	tennis shpeelen
player (m)	der Spieler(-)	derr shpeeler
player (f)	die Spielerin(nen)	dee shpeelerin
playful	verspielt	fer-shpeelt
playground	der Schulhof(¨e)	derr shool-hofe
pleased with	zufrieden mit	tsoofreeden mit
to plow	pflügen	pflewgen
plug (electric)	der Stecker(-)	derr shtecker
plug (bath or sink)	der Stöpsel	derr shto(r)psel
plum	die Pflaume(n)	dee pflaowme(r)
plumber	der Klempner(-)	derr klempner
plus (maths)	und	oont
pocket	die Tasche(n)	dee tashe(r)
poem	das Gedicht(e)	dass gedikht
poetry	Gedichte (pl)	gedikhte(r)
polar bear	der Eisbär(en)	derr ice-bear
police	die Polizei	dee politsye
police car	das Polizeiauto(s)	dass politsye-owto
police station	die Polizeiwache(n)	dee politsye-vakhe(r)
policeman	der Polizist(en)	derr politsist
policewoman	die Polizistin(nen)	dee politsistin
polite	höflich	ho(r)flikh
politics	die Politik	dee politik
pond	der Teich(e)	derr tykh
popular	beliebt	beleebt
port	der Hafen(¨)	derr ha-fen
porter (in hotel)	der Portier(s)	derr port-yay
porter (in airport, station...)	der Gepäckträger(-)	derr gepeck-trayger
porthole	das Bullauge(n)	dass boll-owge(r)
to post	einwerfen	yne-verfen
post office	das Postamt(¨er)	dass post-amt
post-box	der Briefkasten(¨)	derr brief-kasten
postcard	die Postkarte(n)	dee post-karte(r)
postman	der Briefträger(-)	derr brief-trayger
postwoman	die Briefträgerin(nen)	dee brief-traygerin
potato	die Kartoffel(n)	dee kartoffel
to pour	gießen	geess-en
powerboat	das Motorboot(e)	dass motor-boat
prescription	das Rezept(e)	dass re-tsept
present (now)	die Gegenwart	dee gaygen-vart
present (gift)	das Geschenk(e)	dass geshenk
president (m)	der Präsident(en)	derr president
president (f)	die Präsidentin(nen)	dee presidentin
pretty	hübsch	hewbsh
price	der Preis(e)	derr price
prime minister (m)	der Bundeskanzler(-)	derr boondes-kantsler
prime minister (f)	die Bundeskanzlerin(nen)	dee boondes-kantslerin
programme	die Sendung(en)	dee zendoong
pudding	das Dessert(s)	das dessert
puddle	die Pfütze(n)	dee pfewtse(r)
to take someone's pulse	den Puls fühlen	dayn poolss fewlen
to pull	ziehen	tsee-en
pupil (m)	der Schüler(-)	derr shewler
pupil (f)	die Schülerin(nen)	dee shewlerin
puppy	der junge Hunde	derr yoonge(r) hoont
purple	lila	leela
purr	schnurren	shnoorren
purse	die Geldbörse(n)	dee gelt-bo(r)se(r)
to push	drücken	drewken
to put down	hinstellen	hin-shtellen
to put money in, to pay money in	Geld einzahlen	gelt yne-tsahlen

pajamas	der Schlafanzug(¨e)	derr shlaf-antsoog

Q

a quarter	das Viertel(-)	das feertel
a quarter past 10	Viertel nach zehn	feertel nakh tsayn
a quarter to 10	Viertel vor zehn	feertel for tsayn
to ask a question	etwas fragen	etvass fra-gen
quiet, calm	ruhig	roo-ig
quilt	das Federbett(en)	dass fayder-bet

R

race, racing	das Rennen(n)	dass rennen
rabbit	das Kaninchen(-)	dass kaneen-khen
racket	der Schläger(-)	der shlayger
radiator	der Heizkörper(-)	derr hyts-ko(r)per
railway	die Eisenbahn	dee yzen-bahn
rain	der Regen	der raygen
rainbow	der Regenbogen(-)	derr raygen-bogen
raincoat	der Regenmantel(¨)	derr raygen-mantel
raindrop	der Regentropfen(-)	derr raygen-tropfen
to rain	regnen	raygnen
It's raining.	Es regnet.	ess raygnet
rake	die Harke(n)	dee harke(r)
raspberry	die Himbeere(n)	dee heembayre(r)
raw	roh	ro
razor	der Rasierapparat(e)	derr razeer-apparat
to read	lesen	layzen
to read a book	ein Buch lesen	yne bookh layzen
to read a story	eine Geschichte vorlesen	yne(r) geshikhte(r) forlayzen
It's ready. (meal)	Das Essen ist fertig.	dass essen ist fertig
receipt	die Quittung(en)	dee kveetoong
to receive	bekommen	bekommen
receiver	der Telefonhörer(-)	derr telephone-ho(r)-rer
reception	der Empfang	derr empfang
recipe	das Rezept(e)	dass retsept
record	die Platte(n)	dee platte(r)
record player	der Plattenspieler(-)	derr platten-shpeeler
record shop	das Schallplattengeschäft(e)	dass shallplatten-gesheft
rectangle	das Rechteck	dass rekht-eck
red	rot	rote
red hair	rotes Haar	rot-ez har
reed	das Schilf	dass shilf
referee	der Schiedsrichter(-)	derr sheeds-rikhter
to be related to	verwandt sein mit	fervant zyne mit
to reserve	reservieren	reserveeren
to reserve a room	ein Zimmer reservieren	yne tsimmer reserveeren
to reserve a seat	einen Platz reservieren	ynen plats reserveeren
reserved seat	der reservierte Platz	derr reserveerte plats
to rest	sich ausruhen	zikh ows-roohen
restaurant	das Restaurant(s)	dass restaurant
to retire	aufhören zu arbeiten	owf-hu(e)-en tsoo arbytten
by return of post	postwendend	post-vendend
return ticket	die Rückfahrkarte(n)	dee rewk-far-karte(r)
rice	der Reis	derr rice
to ride a bicycle	mit dem Rad fahren	mit daym far-rat fa-ren
on the right	rechts	rekhts
right side	die rechte Seite	dee rekhte zyte(r)
right wing	konservativ	konservateef
ring	der Ring(e)	derr ring
to ring	läuten	loyten
to ring the bell	klingeln	klin-geln
ripe	reif	rife
river	der Fluss(¨e)	derr flooss
to roar	brüllen	brewlen
robe	der Morgenmantel(¨)	derr morgen-mantle
rock	der Felsen(-)	derr felzen
roll	das Brötchen(-)	dass bro(e)t-khen
roof	das Dach(¨er)	dass dakh
room	das Zimmer(-)	dass tsimmer
double-room	das Doppelzimmer(-)	dass dopple-tsimmer
single room	das Einzelzimmer(-)	das eynzel-tsimmer
rose	die Rose(n)	dee rose(r)
to row	rudern	roodern
rowing boat	dass Ruderboot(e)	dass rooder-boat
to rub your eyes	sich die Augen reiben	zikh dee owgen rypen
rubber	der Radiergummi(s)	derr radeer-goomee
rucksack, backpack	der Rucksack(¨e)	derr rook-zack oon-ho(e)flikh
rude	unhöflich	
ruler	das Lineal(e)	dass lin-e-ahl
to run	laufen	lowfen
to run a bath	das Badewasser einlaufen lassen	dass bahde(r)-vasser yne-lowfen lassen
to run away	weglaufen	veck-lowfen
runway	die Landebahn(en)	dee lande(r)-bahn
Russia	Russland	rooss-lant

S

safety belt	der Sicherheitsgurt(e)	derr zikher-hytes-goort
sailor	der Seemann (die Seeleute)	dee zeeloyte(r)
salad	der Salat(e)	derr zalat
salami	die Salami	dee zalami
sale (in shop)	der Schlussverkauf(¨e)	derr shlooss-ferkowf
sales representative (m)	der Vertreter(-)	derr fertrayter
sales representative (f)	die Vertreterin(ne)	dee fertrayterin
salt	das Salz	dass zalts
same	gleich	glykh
the same age as	genauso alt wie	genow zo alt vee
sand	der Sand	derr zant
sandal	die Sandale(n)	dee zandale(r)
sandcastle	die Sandburg(en)	dee zant-boorg
satchel	die Schultasche(n)	dee shool-tashe(r)
Saturday	Samstag	zamstahg

saucepan	der Kochtopf("e)	derr kokh-topf
saucer	die Untertasse(n)	dee oonter-tasse(r)
sausage	die Wurst("e)	dee voorst
saw	die Säge(n)	dee zayge(r)
to say	sagen	zahgen
scales	die Waage(n)	dee vahge(r)
Scandinavia	Skandinavien	scandinah-vien
scarecrow	die Vogelscheuche(n)	dee fogel-shoykhe(r)
scarf	der Schal(s)	derr shahl
scenery	das Bühnenbild(er)	dass bewnen-bilt
school	die Schule(n)	dee shoole(r)
at school	in der Schule	in derr shoole(r)
high school	das Gymnasium (die Gymnasien)	dass gewm-nazium
nursery school	der Kindergarten(")	derr kindergarten
at nursery school	im Kindergarten	im kindergarten
primary school	die Grundschule(n)	dee groont-shoole(r)
scissors	die Schere(n)	dee shayre(r)
to score a goal	ein Tor schießen	yne tore sheesen
screwdriver	der Schraubenzieher(-)	derr shraowben-tsee-er
sea	das Meer(e)	dass mayr
seagull	die Möwe(n)	dee mo(r)ve(r)
to be seasick	seekrank sein	zeh-krank zyne
at the seaside	am Meer	am mayr
season	die Jahreszeit(en)	dee yahrez-tsyte
season ticket	die Zeitkarte(n)	dee tsyte-karte(r)
seat	der Platz("e)	derr plats
reserved seat	der reservierte Platz	derr reser-veerte(r) plats
seaweed	der Seetang	derr zay-tang
second (unit of time)	die Sekunde(n)	dee zekoonde(r)
second	zweite	tsvyte(r)
the second	der, die, das zweite	derr, dee, das tsvyte(r)
second class	die zweite Klasse	dee tsvyte(r) klasse(r)
second floor	der zweite Stock	derr tsvyte(r) shtock
secretary (m)	der Sekretär(e)	derr zekreter
secretary (f)	die Sekretärin(nen)	dee zekreterin
to see	sehen	zayen
See you later.	Bis bald.	biss balt
seed	der Blumensamen(-)	derr bloomen-zahmen
to sell	verkaufen	fer-kkowfen
to send	schicken	shicken
I am sending (...) separately.	Mit getrennter Post erhältst du...	mit getrennter post erhelst doo
to send a postcard	eine Ansichtskarte schicken	yne(r) anzikhts-karte(r) shicken
to send a telegram	ein Telegramm schicken	yne telegram shicken
sentence	der Satz("e)	derr zats
September	September	september
to serve (a meal)	servieren	zerveeren
to serve (in a sport)	aufschlagen	owf-shlahgen
service	die Bedienung	dee bedeenoong
Is service included?	Mit Bedienung?	mit bedeenoong
Service is not included.	Ohne Bedienung.	ohne(r) bedeenoong
seven	sieben	zeeben
seventeen	siebzehn	zeeb-tsyn
seventy	siebzig	zeeb-tsig
to sew	nähen	nay-en
shade	der Schatten(-)	derr shatten
to shake hands with	die Hand schütteln	dee hant shewteln
shallow	flach	flakh
shampoo	das Shampoo(s)	dass shampoo
shape	die Form(en)	dee form
to shave	sich rasieren	zikh razeeren
electric shaver	der elektrische Rasierapparat	derr elektrishe(r) razeer-apparat
shaving foam	der Rasierschaum	derr razeer-shaowm
sheep	das Schaf(e)	dass shahf
sheepdog	der Hütehund(e)	derr hewte(r)-hoont
sheet	das Bettlaken(-)	dass bet-lahken
shell	die Muscheln(n)	dee mooshel
to shine	scheinen	shynen
ship	das Schiff(e)	dass shiff
shirt	das Hemd(en)	dass hemt
shoe	der Schuh(e)	derr shoe
gym shoe	Die Turnschuhe (pl)	dee toorn-shoe-e(r)
shop	das Geschäft(e)	dass gesheft
shop assistant (m)	der Verkäufer(-)	derr ferkoy-fer
shop assistant (f)	die Verkäuferin(nen)	dee ferkoy-ferin
shopkeeper (m)	der Ladenbesitzer(-)	derr lahden-bezitser
shopkeeper (f)	die Ladenbesitzerin(nen)	dee lahden-bezitserin
shop window	das Schaufenster(-)	dass shaowfenster
to shop at the market	auf dem Markt einkaufen	owf daym markt yne-kowfen
to go shopping	einkaufen gehen	yne-kowfen gay-en
shopping bag	die Einkaufstausche(n)	dee yne-kowfs-tashe(r)
shopping cart	der Einkaufswagen(-)	derr yne-kowfss-vahgen
to be short	klein sein	klyne zyne
shoulder	die Schulter(n)	dee shoolter
to shout	rufen	roofen
shower	die Dusche(n)	dee doosher(r)
to have a shower	duschen	dooshen
with shower	mit Dusche	mit dooshe
shut	geschlossen	geshlossen
shy	schüchtern	skewkhtern
side	die Seite(n)	dee zyte(r)
sidewalk	der Bürgersteig(e)	derr bewrg-er-shtyge
to sightsee	etwas besichtigen	etvass bezikhtigen
signpost	das Hinweisschild(er)	dass hin-vyss-shilt
silly	albern	al-bern
silver	das Silber	dass zilber
made of silver	aus Silber	owss zilber
to sing	singen	zingen
to sing out of tune	falsch singen	falsh zingen
singer (m)	der Sänger(-)	derr zenger
singer (f)	die Sängerin(nen)	dee zengerin
single room	das Einzelzimmer(-)	dass yntsel-tsimmer
sink	die Spüle	dee shpewle(r)
sister	die Schwester(n)	dee shwester
to sit an exam	eine Prüfung machen	yn(e) prwfong makhen
to sit by the fire	am Kamin sitzen	am kameen zitsen
to sit down	sich setzen	zikh zetsen
to be sitting down	sitzen	zitsen
six	sechs	zex
sixteen	sechzehn	zekh-tsayn
sixty	sechzig	zekh-tsig
size	die Größe(n)	dee gru(e)sse(r)

What size is this?	Welche Größe ist es?	velkhe gru(r)sse(r) ist es
skis	die Skier (pl)	dee shee-er
ski boots	die Skistiefel (pl)	dee shee-shteefel
ski instructor (m)	der Skilehrer(-)	derr shee-layrer
ski instructor (f)	die Skilehrerin(nen)	dee shee-layrerin
ski pole	der Skistock("e)	derr shee-shtock
ski resort	der Skiort(e)	derr shee-ort
ski slope, ski run	der Hang("e)	derr hang
to go skiing	zum Skilaufen gehen	tsoom shee-lawfen gayen
skilled, good with your hands	geschickt	geshickt
skin	die Haut	dee howt
skirt	der Rock("e)	derr rock
sky	der Himmel	derr himmel
skyscraper	der Wolkenkratzer	derr volken-kratser
sled	der Schlitten(en)	derr shlitten
to sleep	schlafen	shlahfen
Sleep well.	Schlaf gut.	shlahf goot
sleeping-car	der Schlafwagen(-)	derr shlahf-vahgen
sleeping ag	der Schlafsack("e)	derr shlahf-zakc
to be sleepy	schläfrig sein	shlayfrig zyne
slide	die Rutschbahn(en)	dee rootsh-bahn
slim	schlank	shlank
to slip	ausrutschen	owss-rootshen
slippers	die Hausschuhe (pl)	dee house-shoe-e(r)
slope	der Hang("e)	derr hang
slow	langsam	langzam
small	klein	klyne
small (clothes size)	klein	klyne
to smile	lächeln	lekheln
smoke	der Rauch	derr rowkh
smoke stack (ship)	der Schornstein(e)	derr shorn-shtyne
snake	die Schlange(n)	dee shlange(r)
to sneeze	niesen	neezen
to snore	schnarchen	shnarkhen
snow	der Schnee	der shnay
It's snowing.	Es schneit.	ess shnyte
snowman	der Schneemann("er)	derr shnay-man
soaked to the skin	klatschnass	klatsh-nass
soap	die Seife(n)	dee zyfe(r)
soccer ball, ball	der Fußball("e)	derr fooss-bal
to play soccer	Fußball spielen	fooss-bal shpeelen
society	die Gesellschaft	dee gezell-shaft
sock	die Socke(n)	dee zocke(r)
sofa	das Sofa(s)	dass zofa
soft	weich	vykh
soil	die Erde	dee erde(r)
soldier	der Soldat(en)	derr zoldat
someone	jemand	yaymant
son	der Sohn("e)	derr zone
only son	der einzige Sohn	derr yntsige(r) zone
to sort, to sort out, to arrange	sortieren	zorteeren
soup	die Suppe(n)	dee zoope(r)
sour, sharp	sauer	zaower
south	der Süden	derr zewden
South America	Südamerika	zewd-america
South Pole	der Südpol	derr zewd-pole
to sow	säen	zey-en
space	der Weltraum	derr velt-raowm
spaceship	das Raumschiff(e)	dass raowm-shif
spade	der Spaten(-)	der shpahten
spade (shovel or child's spade)		
Spain	Spanien	shpahnien
Spanish (language or subject)	Spanisch	spahnish
sparrow	der Spatz(en)	derr shpats
spelling	die Rechtschreibung	dee rekht-shryboong
to spend money	Geld ausgeben	glet owss-gayben
spice	das Gewürz	dass gewewrts
spider	die Spinne(n)	dee shpeenne(r)
spinach	der Spinat	derr shpinat
to splash	spritzen	shpritsen
spoon	der Löffel(-)	derr lo(r)ffel
sport	der Sport	derr shport
sports equipment (section in shop)	die Sportabteilung(en)	dee shport-aptyloong
spotlight	der Scheinwerfer(-)	derr shine-verfer
spotted	gepunktet	gepoonktet
to sprain your wrist	sich die Hand verstauchen	zikh dee hant-fershtaowken
spring	der Frühling	derr frewling
square (shape)	das Quadrat(e)	das kvadrat
square (in a town)	der Platz("e)	der plats
to play squash	Squash spielen	squash shpeelen
squirrel	das Eichhörnchen	dass ykh-ho(r)n-khen
stable	der Pferdestall("e)	derr pferde(r)-shtal
stage (theatre)	die Bühne(n)	dee bewne(r)
staircase (stairs)	die Treppen(n)	dee treppe(r)
stamp	die Briefmarke(n)	dee brief-marke(r)
to stand up	aufstehen	owf-shta-yen
to be standing	stehen	shtay-en
star	der Stern(e)	derr shtern
to start off (a vehicle)	losfahren	loss-fahren
starter (meal)	die Vorspeise(n)	dee fore-shpyze(r)
statue	die Statue(n)	dee shtatoo-e(r)
to stay in a hotel	im Hotel wohnen	im hotel vo-nen
steak	das Steak(s)	dass steak
to steal	stehlen	shtaylen
steep	steil	shtyle
steering wheel	das Lenkrad("er)	dass lenk-rat
stewardess	die Stewardess(en)	dee stewardess
to stick	einkleben	yne-klayben
to sting	stechen	shtekhen
stomach	der Bauch("e)	der bowkh
to have stomach-ache	Bauchweh haben	bowkh-vay ha-ben
storm	der Sturm("e)	derr shtoorm
story	die Geschichte(n)	dee geshikhte(r)
stove	der Kocher(-)	derr kokher
straight (for hair)	glatt	glatt
straight hair	glattes Haar	glatt-ez hahr
to go straight on	geradeaus weiterfahren	ge-rade(r)-owss vyter-fahren
strawberry	die Erdbeere(n)	dee ert-bayre(r)
stream	der Bach("e)	der bakh
street	die Straße(n)	dee shtrasse(r)
street light	die Straßenlaterne(n)	dee shtrassen-laterne(r)
stroller	der Sportwagen(-)	derr shport-vahgen
side-street	die Seitenstraße(n)	dee zyten-shtrasse(r)
one way street	die Einbahnstraße(n)	dee yne-bahn-shtrasse(r)
stretch	sich strecken	zikh shtrecken

stretcher	die Bahre(n)	dee bahre(r)	to take off	starten	shtarten
striped	gestreift	ge-stryft	to take out, to draw	abheben	ap-hayben
strong	stark	shtark	to take money out	Geld abheben	gelt ap-hyben
student (m)	der Student(en)	derr shtudent	to be tall	groß sein	gross zyne
student (f)	die Studentin(nnen)	dee shtudentin	tame	zahm	tsahm
to study	studieren	shtoodeeren	tanned	braun	brawn
subject (of study)	das Fach(¨er)	dass fakh	tap	der Wasserhahn(e)	derr vasser-hahn
suburb	der Vorort(e)	derr for-ort	to tap your feet	den Takt mitklopfen	dayn takt mit-klopfen
subway	die Unterführung(en)	dee oonter-fewroong	tart, flan (small)	das Obsttörtchen	dass opst-to(r)rt-khen
subway (train)	die U-Bahn(en)	dee oo-bahn	taste, flavor	der Geschmack	derr geshmack
subway station	die U-Bahnstation(en)	dee oo-bahn-shtats-yoan	to taste, to try	probieren	probeeren
sugar	der Zucker	der tsooker	It tastes good.	Das schmeckt gut.	das shmeckt goot
suitcase	der Koffer(-)	derr koffer	tax	die Steuer(n)	dee shtoyer
summer	der Sommer	derr zommer	taxi	das Taxi(s)	dass taxi
summit	der Gipfel(-)	derr gipfel	to hail a taxi	ein Taxi rufen	yne taxi roofen
sun	die Sonne	dee zonne(r)	tea	der Tee	derr tay
The sun is shining.	Die Sonne scheint.	dee zonne(r) shynt	tea towel	das Geschirrtuch(¨er)	dass gesheer-tookh
to sunbathe	sonnenbaden	zonnen-bahden	to teach	lehren	layren
Sunday	Sonntag (m)	zonn-tahg	teacher (m)	der Lehrer(-)	derr layrer
sunglasses	die Sonnenbrille(n)	dee zonnen-brille(r)	teacher (f)	die Lehrerin(nen)	dee layrerin
sunrise	der Sonnenaufgang(¨e)	derr zonnen-owf-gang	team	die Mannschaft(en)	dee man-shaft
sunset	der Sonnenuntergang(¨e)	derr zonnen-oonter-gang	teapot	die Teekanne(n)	dee tay-kanne(r)
sunshade	der Sonnenschirm(e)	der zonnen-sheerm	to tear	zerreißen	tser-ryssen
sun lotion	das Sonnenschutzmittel(-)	dass zonnen-shoots-mittel	telegram	das Telegramm(e)	dass telegram
supermarket	der Supermarkt(¨e)	derr zupermarkt	telephone	das Telefon(e)	dass telephone
to go to the supermarket	in den Supermarkt gehen	in dayn zupermarkt gay-en	telephone area code	die Vorwahl	dee vor-vahl
supper	das Abendessen(-)	dass ahbend-essen	telephone box	die Telefonzelle(n)	dee telephone-tselle(r)
surgeon (m)	der Chirurg(en)	der sheeroorg	telephone directory	das Telefonbuch(¨er)	dass telephone-bookh
surgeon (f)	die Chirurgin(nen)	dee sheeroorgin	telephone number	die Telefonnummer(n)	dee telephone-noomer
surname	der Nachname(n)	derr nakh-nahme(r)	to answer the telephone	ans Telefon gehen	anss telephone gay-en
to sweat	schwitzen	shvitsen	to make a telephone call	telefonieren	telephoneeren
sweater	der Pullover(-)	derr pulover	telescope	das Fernrohr	dass fern-raor
sweet, charming	süß	zewss	television	der Fernseher(-)	der fern-zayer
sweet (sugar)	süß	zewss	to have a temperature	Fieber haben	feeber ha-ben
sweet (smelling)	duftend	dooftend	to take someone's temperature	die Temperatur messen	dee temartoor messen
to swim	schwimmen	shvimmen	ten	zehn	tseyn
to have a swim, to go in	ins Wasser gehen	ins vasser gay-en	tenant (m)	der Mieter(-)	derr meeter
swimming pool	das Schwimmbad(¨er)	dass shvimm-baht	tenant (f)	die Mieterin(nen)	dee meeterin
swing	die Schaukel(n)	dee showkel	tennis	das Tennis	dass tennis
to switch off	ausschalten	owss-shalten	tennis court	der Tennisplatz(¨e)	derr tennis-plats
to switch the light on	das Licht anmachen	das likht an-makhen	to play tennis	Tennis spielen	tennis shpeelen
Switzerland	die Schweiz	dee shvyts	tent	das Zelt(e)	dass tselt
			term	das Schulhalbjahr	dass shool-hlap-yahr

T

table	der Tisch(e)	derr tish	to thank	sich bedanken	zikh bedanken
beside table	der Nachttisch(e)	derr nakht-tish	Thank your for your letter of...	Vielen Dank für ihren Brief vom...	feelen dank fewr eeren brief fom
to lay the table	den Tisch decken	den tish decken	Thank you very much.	Danke schön.	danke(r) sho(r)n
tablecloth	die Tischdeck(en)	dee tish-decke(r)	That will be/cost...	Das macht...	dass makht
tail	der Schwanz(¨e)	derr shvants	to thaw	tauen	taowen
to take	nehmen	naymen	theatre	das Theater(-)	dass tay-ahter
to take the bus	mit dem Bus fahren	mit daym booss fa-ren	then	damals	da-mals
to take a photograph	ein Foto machen	yne photo makhen	thermometer	das Thermometer(-)	dass termo-mayter
to take someone's pulse	den Puls fühlen	dayn pools fewlen	thin	dünn	dewn
to take someone's temperature	die Temperatur messen	dee temeratoor messen	a third	das Drittel(-)	dass drittel
			the third	der, die, das dritte	derr, dee, dass dritte(r)
			thirteen	dreizehn	dry-tsayn
			thirty	dreißig	dry-sig
			to be thirsty	Durst haben	doorst ha-ben
			this evening	heute Abend	hoyte(r) ahbend

this morning	heute Morgen	hoyte(r) morgen
a thousand	tausend	toawzend
thread	der Faden(¨)	derr fa-den
three	drei	dry
three quarters	Dreiviertel	dry-feertel
through	durch (acc)	doorkh
to throw	werfen	verfen
thrush	die Drossel(n)	dee drossel
thumb	der Daumen(-)	derr dowmen
thunder	der Donner	derr donner
Thursday	Donnerstag (m)	donners-tahg
ticket	die Fahrkarte(n)	dee fahr-karte(r)
airline ticket	der Flugschein(e)	derr floog-shine
platform ticket	die Bahnsteigkarte(n)	dee bahn-shtyg-karte(r)
return ticket	die Rückfahrkarte(n)	dee rewk-fahr-karte(r)
ticket collector	der Fahrkarten-automat(en)	derr fahr-karten-owtomat
ticket office	der Fahrkartenschalter(-)	derr fahr-karten-shalter
to tidy up	aufräumen	owf-roymen
tie	die Krawatte(n)	dee kravatte(r)
tiger	der Tiger(-)	derr teeger
tight	eng	eng
tights	die Strumpfhose(n)	dee shtroompf-hoze(r)
time	die Zeit	dee tsyte
on time	pünktlich	pewnkt-likh
to be on time	pünktlich sein	pewnkt-likh zyne
What time is it?	Wie spät ist es?	vee shpayt ist ess
times (maths)	mal	mal
timetable (for pupils and students)	der Stundenplan(¨e)	derr shtooden-plan
timetable (for transport)	der Fahrplan(¨e)	derr fahr-plan
tiny	winzig	vintsig
tip	das Trinkgeld(er)	dass trink-gelt
tire	der Reifen	der ryfen
to have a flat tire	einen Platten haben	ynen platten ha-ben
to, towards	auf ... (acc) zu	owf ... tsoo
today	heute	hoyte(r)
toe	der Zeh(en)	derr tsay
together	zusammen	tsoo-zammen
toilet	die Toilette(n)	dee twalette(r)
tomato	die Tomate(n)	dee tomate(r)
tomorrow	morgen	morgen
tomorrow evening	morgen Abend	morgen ahbend
tomorrow morning	morgen früh	morgen frew
tongue	die Zunge(n)	dee tsoonge(r)
tooth	der Zahn(¨e)	derr tsahn
to have toothache	Zahnschmerzen haben	tsahn-shmersten ha-ben
toothpaste	die Zahnpasta	dee tsahn-pasta
turtle	die Schildkröte	dee shilt-kro(r)te(r)
to touch	berühren	berewren
tour bus	der Reisebus(se)	derr ryze(r) booss
tourist (m)	der Tourist(en)	derr too-rist
tourist (f)	die Touristin(nen)	dee too-ristin
towel	das Handtuch(¨er)	das hant-tookh
town	die Stadt(¨e)	dee shtat
town hall	das Rathaus(¨er)	dass rat-house
town square	die Innenstadt(¨e)	dee innen-shtat
toy, toys	das Spielzeug	das shpeel-tsoyg
toys (section in shop)	Spielwaren	shpeel-va-ren
track	die Gleise (pl)	dee glyze(r)
tracksuit	der Trainingsanzug(¨e)	derr trainings-antsoog
tractor	der Trecker(-)	derr trecker
trade union	die Gewerkschaft(en)	dee geverk-shaft
traffic	der Verkehr	derr fer-kehr
traffic jam	der Stau(s)	derr staow
traffic lights	die Ampel(n)	dee ampel
train	der Zug(¨e)	derr tsoog
The train from...	Der Zug aus...	derr tsoog owss
The train to...	Der Zug nach...	derr tsooh nakh
intercity train	der Intercity	der intercity
goods train	der Güterzug(¨e)	derr gewter-tsoog
trash can	der Papierkorb(¨e)	derr papeer-korp
to travel by boat	mit dem Schiff fahren	mit daym shiff fa-ren
traveler (m/f)	der/die Reisende(n)	derr/dee ryzende(r)
tray	das Tablett(s)	dass ta-peltt
tree	der Baum(¨e)	derr baowm
triangle	das Dreieck(e)	dass dry-eck
trowel	die Schaufel(n)	dee showfel
truck	der Lastwagen(-)	derr last-vagen
truck driver	der Lastenwagenfahrer(-)	derr lastvagen-fahrer
true	wahr	var
trumpet	die Trompete(n)	dee trompayte(r)
to play the trumpet	Trompete spielen	trompayte(r) shpeelen
trunk (elephant's)	der Rüssel(-)	derr rewssel
trunk (of car)	der Stiefel(-)	derr shteefel
T-Shirt	das T-Shirt(s)	dass t-shirt
Tuesday	Dienstag (m)	deens-tahg
Tuesday, the second of June	Dienstag, der zweite Juni	deens-tahg, derr tsvyte(r) joonee
tulip	die Tulpe(n)	dee toolpe(n)
tune	die Melodie(n)	dee meload-ee
to turn	abbiegen	ap-beegen
to turn left	links abbiegen	links ap-beegen
to turn right	rechts abbiegen	rekhts ap-beegen
tusk	der Stoßzahn(¨e)	derr shtoass-tsahn
twelve	zwölf	tsvo(r)lf
twenty	zwanzig	tsvantsig
twin (brother or sister)	der Zwilling(e)	derr tsvilling
two	zwei	tsvye

U

umbrella	der Regenschirm(e)	derr raygen-sheerm
uncle	der Onkel(-)	der onkel
under	unter (acc or dat)	oonter
underpants	die Unterhose(n)	dee oonter-houze(r)
undershirt	das Unterhemd(en)	dass oonter-hemt
to get undressed	sich ausziehen	zikh owss-tsee-en
unemployment	die Arbeitslosigkeit	dee arbyts-lozig-kyte
United States	die USA (pl)	dee oo-ess-ah
universe	das Universum	dass ooniversoom
to unload	ausladen	owss-lahden
up	hinauf (acc)	hin-owf
to get up	aufstehen	ofw-shty-en
upstairs	oben	o-ben

to go upstairs	**nach oben gehen**	*nakh o-ben gay-en*	washing machine	**die Waschmaschine(n)**	*die vash-masheene*
Urgent message stop phone home stop	**Dringend stop sofort zu Hause anrufen stop**	*dringned shtop zofort tsoo howse(r) anroofen shtop*	wasp	**die Wespe**	*dee vespe(r)*
			to watch television	**fernsehen**	*fern-zay-en*
			watch	**die Armbanduhr**	*dee armbant-oor*
useful	**nützlich**	*newtslikh*	mineral water	**das Mineralwasser**	*dass miner-al-vasser*
usherette	**die Platzanweiserin(nen)**	*dee plats-anvyzerin*	watering can	**die Gießkanne(n)**	*dee geess-kanne(r)*

V

			to waterski	**Wasserski laufen**	*vasser-shee-laowfen*
vacation	**der Ulaub(e)**	*der oorlaowp*	wave	**die Welle(n)**	*dee velle(r)*
to go on vacation	**in Urlaub fahren**	*in ooraloowp fa-ren*	to ask the way	**nach dem Weg fragen**	*nakh daym vayg fra-gen*
to vacuum	**staubsaugen**	*shtowb-zowgen*	Which way is...?	**In welcher Richtung ist...?**	*in velkher rikhtoong ist*
valley	**das Tal(¨er)**	*dass tahl*	weak	**schwach**	*shvakh*
van	**der Lieferwagen(-)**	*derr leefer-vahgen*	to wear	**tragen**	*trahgen*
			to wear glasses	**eine Brille tragen**	*yne(r) brille(r) trahgen*
veal	**das Kalbfleisch**	*dass kalp-flysh*	weather	**das Wetter**	*das vetter*
vegetable patch	**das Gemüsebeet(e)**	*dass gemewze(r) beyt*	weather forecast	**die Wettervorhersage(n)**	*dee vetter-fore-her-zahge(r)*
vegetables	**das Gemüse(-)**	*dass gemewze(r)*	What is the weather like?	**Wie ist das Wetter?**	*vee ist dass vetter*
Very well, thank you. (Answer to "How are you?")	**Danke, gut.**	*danke(r), goot*	wedding	**die Hochzeit(en)**	*dee hokh-tsyte*
vicar	**der Pfarrer(-)**	*derr pfarrer*	wedding ring	**der Ehering(e)**	*derr aye(r)-ring*
VCR (video cassette recorder)	**der Videorecorder(-)**	*derr video recorder*	Wednesday	**Mittwoch (m)**	*mit-wokh*
			weed	**das Unkraut(¨er)**	*dass oonkraowt*
video camera	**die Videokamera**	*dee video camera*	to weed	**das Unkraut jäten**	*dass oonkraowt yay-ten*
view	**die Aussicht**	*dee owss-zikht*	week	**die Woche(n)**	*dee vokhe(r)*
village	**das Dorf(¨er)**	*dass dorf*	week-end	**das Wochenende(n)**	*dass vokhen-ende(r)*
vine	**die Rebe(n)**	*dee reybe(r)*	weeping willow	**die Trauerweide(n)**	*dee traower-vyde(r)*
vinegar	**der Essig**	*derr esig*			
vineyard	**der Weinberg(e)**	*derr vine-berg*	to weigh	**wiegen**	*veegen*
violin	**die Geige(n)**	*dee gyge(r)*	to weigh yourself	**sich wiegen**	*zikh veegen*
to play the violin	**Geige spielen**	*gyge(r) shpeeln*	weight	**das Gewicht(e)**	*dass gevikht*
volume	**der Inhalt(e)**	*derr inhalt*	well	**gut**	*goot*
to vomit	**sich übergeben**	*zikh ewber-gayben*	to have eaten well	**gut gegessen haben**	*goot gegessen ha-ben*
to vote	**wählen**	*vaylen*	Very well, thank you. (answer to "How are you")	**Danke, gut.**	*danke(r), goot*

W

			wellington boots	**die Gummistiefel (pl)**	*dee goomee-shteefel*
to wag its tail	**mit dem Schwanz wedeln**	*mit daym shvants veydeln*	west	**der Westen**	*derr vesten*
wages	**der Lohn(¨e)**	*derr loan*	What is the weather like?	**Wie ist das Wetter?**	*vee ist dass vetter*
to wait for	**warten auf**	*varten owf*	What size is this?	**Welche Größe es?**	*velkhe(r) gru(r)sse(r) ist ess*
waiter	**der Ober(-)**	*derr o-ber*			
waiting room	**der Wartesaal(¨e)**	*der varte(r)-zahl*	What time is it?	**Wie spät es es?**	*vee shpayt ist ess*
to wake up	**aufwachen**	*owf-vakhen*	What's your name?	**Wie heißt du?**	*vee hysst doo*
to go for a walk	**spazieren gehen**	*shpatseeren gay-en*	What would you like?	**Was hätten Sie gerne?**	*vass hetten zee gerne(r)*
to walk	**gehen**	*gay-en*	wheel	**das Rad(¨er)**	*dass raht*
to walk barefoot	**barfuß gehen**	*barfooss gay-en*	wheelbarrow	**die Schubkarre(n)**	*dee shoob-karre(r)*
to take the dog for a walk	**den Hund ausführen**	*dayn hoont owss-fewren*	Which way is...?	**in welcher Richtung ist...?**	*in velkher rikhtoong ist*
wall	**die Wand(¨e)**	*dee vant*	to whisper	**flüstern**	*flewstern*
wallet	**die Brieftasche(n)**	*dee brief-tashe(r)*	white	**weiß**	*vyss*
			width	**die Breite(n)**	*dee bryte)r)*
wall-to-wall carpet	**der Teppichboden**	*derr teppich-boden*	wife	**die Ehefrau(en)**	*dee aye(r)-fraow*
			wild	**wild**	*vilt*
to wash, to have a wash	**sich waschen**	*zikh vashen*	wild flowers	**die Wiesenblumen (pl)**	*dee veezen-bloomen*
to wash your hair	**sich die Haare waschen**	*zikh dee hahre(r) vashen*	to win	**gewinnen**	*gevinnen*
			wind	**der Wind**	*derr vint*
washcloth	**der Waschlappen(-)**	*der vash-lappen*	window	**das Fenster**	*dass fenster*
washing line	**die Wäscheleine(n)**	*dee veshe(r) line(r)*			

to go window-shopping	einen Schaufensterbummel machen	ynen shaow-fenster-boomel makhen
window display, shop window	das Schaufenster(-)	dass shaow-fenster
windshield	die Windschutzscheibe(n)	dee vint-shoots-shybe(r)
to windsurf	windsurfen	vint-surfen
It's windy.	Es ist windig.	ess ist vindig
wine	der Wein(e)	der vine
wing	der Flügel(-)	derr flewgel
winter	der Winter	derr vinter
to wipe	abtrocknen	ap-trocknen
Wish you were here.	Schade, dass du nicht hier bist.	shahde(r), dass doo nikht here bist
with	mit (dat)	mit
with balcony	mit Balkon	mit balcone
with shower	mit Dusche	mit dooshe(r)
without	ohne (acc)	ohne(r)
woman	die Frau(en)	dee fraow
wood	der Wald("er)	der valt
wooden, made of wood	aus Holz	ows holts
woodwork	das Tischlern	dass tishlern
woolen	aus Wolle	owss volle(r)
word	das Wort("er)	dass vort
to work	arbeiten	arbyten
to go to work	zur Arbeit gehen	tsoor arbyte gay-en
world	die Welt(en)	dee velt
I would like...	Ich hätte gern...	ikh hette(r) gern
wrapping	die Verpackung(en)	dee ferpackoong
to write	schreiben	shryben
to write a check	einen Scheck ausstellen	ynen sheck owss-stellen
to write a letter	einen Brief schreiben	ynen brief shryben
wrist	das Handgelenk(e)	dass hant-gelenk
writing paper	das Schreibpapier	dass shrybe-papeer

Y

yarn	die Wolle	dee volle(r)
to yawn	gähnen	gaynen
year	das Jahr(e)	dass yar
yellow	gelb	gelp
yes	ja	ya
yesterday	gestern	gestern
yesterday evening	gestern Abend	gestern ahbend
yesterday morning	gestern Morgen	gestern morgen
yogurt	das Joghurt(s)	dass yo-goort
young	jung	yoong
younger than	jünger als	yewnger alss
Yours faithfully	Mit freundlichen Grüßen	mit froyntlikhen grewssen

Z

zebra	das Zebra(s)	dass tsayr-bra
zero	null	nool
zip code	die Postleitzahl	dee ost-lyt-tsahl
zipper	der Reißverschluss	der rice-fershlooss
zoo	der Zoo(s)	derr tso
zoo keeper	der Wärter(-)	derr verter

First published in 1988 by Usborne Publishing L
Usborne House, 83-85 Saffron Hill,
London EC1N 8RT, England. www.usborne.com
Copyright © 2003, 1988 Usborne Publishing Ltd

Printed in Great Britain.